NEWBORN CARE BASICS:

Baby Care Tips
For New Moms

Author
Lisa Marshall

TABLES OF CONTENTS

THANK YOU FOR PURCHASING THIS BOOK!

Click on this link to download this FREE tool

https://bit.ly/2FAGaqX

Note: If you have purchased the paperback format then you need to write this link on your browser search bar. This tool is a useful resource to understand the development of the language and communication of children.

Subscribe to Our Newsletter and Get a FREE Audiobook!

More information at the end of the book in "Other Books"…

INTRODUCTION

Congratulations on downloading *Newborn Care Basics: Baby Care Tips For New Moms* and thank you for doing so. With as much advice as there is about babies out in the world, this book will be your first step to gain more knowledge about the basics. It is there to help alleviate some of the concerns that you may have as a new parent in those first overwhelming moments. This book will serve as your trusted guide as you watch your baby grow.

The following chapters will discuss the basics regarding newborn care for all parents. Chapter by chapter, it will lead you through the baby's first couple of weeks concerning anything from feeding baby to clothing baby. These chapters include information on bonding, belly button care, and even circumcision without being biased towards anyone's way of raising a baby.

It is the hope that they will be not only informative but that they will be a guide to assuage any fears that may be lingering after the birth of the most precious gift, your baby.

It is in those moments, when parents are feeling their most vulnerable, that a handy guide such as this will be most valuable.

It will also show you that there is no one right way. Babies tend to do things at their own pace and are their own human beings with specific preferences. Some babies sleep, and some do not. Some babies like warm milk, and some like it cold. This does not mean that you as a parent are doing anything incorrectly.

There is also some special information for those parents that have decided to take the journey of parenthood through adoption. It is the journey of raising a baby that makes a person a parent, no matter how someone became that parent. Adoption is a wonderful gift to give to a child in need, and one that is most definitely not given lightly.

There are plenty of books on this subject on the market, thanks again for choosing this one! Every effort was made to ensure it is full of as much useful information as possible, please enjoy it!

CHAPTER 1:

Bonding with Baby

As you begin the miraculous journey of caring for your newborn baby, different questions start to arise. This particular chapter hopes to alleviate any questions that you may have concerning bonding with your baby, a very natural and important process that helps the baby grow to become a fully functioning and loving adult. A bond is what makes a family.

Bonding is the attachment that is formed between a newborn baby and its parents. This bond is the one that allows the family to be in tune with one another, responding to needs as necessary. Through this bond, the parent will know when the child needs something, for instance, helping a mom wake up in the middle of the night to feed the child.

A bond works almost like a communication tool between the parents and the baby. Since a newborn is still too young to speak and make their wishes known, forming a bond with its caregiver is the one way in which the baby can express its wishes. As mentioned, parents become more in tune with the baby ensuring that its needs are fulfilled in a timely fashion.

The most surprising thing about bonding with a baby is how much it actually requires. This is a bond that is formed through fulfilling the baby's needs rather than just by seeing the baby for the first time. Of course, that does happen as well, but most of the time a bond just requires good, hard work.

The Importance of Bonding

This bond is very important to the development of the newest little bundle of joy. When a baby is born, their brains are ready to learn from the moment they sense the world. Their senses will take in all that is around them and expand the most for the first two years of their life.

Studies have been performed that prove that by the time a baby reaches the age of 3, their brain is 90% the size of an adult brain. What this means is that during those first years, their brain is growing the most, including the wiring that it contains. Bonding and consistent human interaction are what assists the brain in building those very important synapses, or connections, within the brain itself.

It has also been proven that newborns should bond with their fathers, and other family members, besides just mom as is usually expected. Various studies have shown that in infants where the father has taken an interest in interacting with them from the start, the baby's development both mentally and physically was significantly enhanced. Kids are also more successful academically if they start developing a bond with dad from the very beginning.

How to Bond with Baby

There are many ways in which the bond with the baby can be enforced. A bond between a baby and its parents can be cultivated from the very beginning even if the baby has to go to the NICU for any reason. Though the bond can be developed between the baby and any of the parents, it will form a little differently in each case as for instance, fathers aren't able to breastfeed which is a great bonding experience for mothers.

Each parent can tailor the bonding experience to themselves and their baby, as obviously not every baby is the same. What may work for one family may not work for another, making the list of possible bonding experiences rather lengthy. One important thing to remember during this experience is to allow it to happen as naturally as possible, there is no need in forcing it.

Bonding with Mothers

A bond with the mother can start from the very moment that the baby is born. During a vaginal delivery, this is done through the use of skin to skin contact. When the baby is born, barring any issues, the baby can be placed right on top of mom's chest to begin the skin to skin and feeding time. It has been proven that most babies will root for mom instinctively, moving down or up her chest as needed to find their sustenance.

Nowadays, most hospitals encourage this skin to skin time, and it should definitely be an option that is explored. When taking a tour around the hospital labor and delivery, it is best to ask the hospital on their policies regarding this very precious time. Plenty of hospitals will ensure that parents do not get disturbed by anyone during these vital moments, for up to an hour or two after the birth.

Skin to skin is even something that is a possibility for a mom that has delivered via cesarean section. In instances where the mom has a spinal block or an epidural, barring all complications, nurses or the support purse is able to place the baby by the mother's head during the remaining portion of the surgery. This allows the mom and baby to start getting to know each other before she is able to hold the baby on her own. Once that is a possibility, most likely during recovery, the baby will continue the rest of the bonding process through skin to skin and feeding.

Even in an instance where the laboring mother needs to be placed under general anesthesia, bonding is possible. The timeline of the start of bonding will most likely be pushed back somewhat, but it is still something that can be strived for. It is important to remember to speak with the nurses that are providing the care to ensure that all expectations are met. This will ensure that when the mother is united with the baby, enough bonding time is secured.

From there, whether at home or in the hospital, a mother will have plenty of opportunities to bond with the baby. One of the most common ways in which a baby will start to form that bond is through feeding. That bond will develop whether the baby is breast or formula-fed as it is also about the closeness of the act itself. Babies who are breastfeeding, when awake, will stare in the eyes of their mother. If a baby is bottle-fed, the mother should ensure that she is still providing that closeness. This means that whether bottle-fed or not, a mother should limit doing anything else when she is feeding her baby, but look back into their eyes.

If a mother is breastfeeding, she also has the added benefit of taking what is called a "nursing vacation". This does not mean a vacation from nursing, but rather a weekend-long stay in bed with the baby where the baby is free to explore and nurse on demand. Even if a weekend is not a feasible option, it is a good bonding experience for both mom and the baby to lay beside each other without any clothes and feel closeness.

Bonding with Fathers

Contrary to popular belief, newborns also need to start bonding with their father from the very beginning. The original school of thought was that at the very beginning, and even throughout most of childhood, a father was not needed. It was always the mother who took care of the children and the household; therefore, fathers never truly began to bond with their children.

Recent studies, however, have shown that if a child begins the bonding process right away, there are surprising benefits. Those benefits are not only for the baby, but they extend to the father as well. The necessary bonding can begin right after the baby's birth whether the mother has had a c-section or a vaginal delivery in the form of skin to skin.

Much as the mother gets the skin to skin time, it can be the couple's decision to provide that time for the father as well. This can take place still in recovery, or it can take place at a much later time, however, it is something that is encouraged for both parents.

Since there will be family members who would also like to meet the bundle of joy, the father can make the conscious effort to bond with the baby after the baby is settled at home. There are many different ways that this bonding can continue such as through assisting with feeds. A baby will bond through feeding through physical and eye contact, something that the father can also provide.

Bonding Tips

There are various ways in which bonding with both parents can continue. Though a baby may be small in the beginning and will more often than not sleep most of the day away, it is important to provide as much contact as possible when the baby is awake or feeding. Both parents can share responsibilities equally if that is at all possible.

As soon as the baby begins to be more aware of their surroundings, parents are encouraged to participate in other stimulation such as through making silly faces or taking walks. Even something as simple as a diaper change, performed by either parent, assists in growing that necessary bond. Some small ways in which parents can bond with their baby include:

- Giving the baby a very gentle massage. This can be done either with a bath or without
- Reading books
- Kiss baby as often as you'd like
- Wearing the baby either out of the house or in while doing chores
- Looking into their eyes
- Sing to the baby
- Sleep close to the baby within the safe sleep practices that will be covered later in the book

- Always respond to the baby's cries promptly
- Play with the baby making facial expression or coos
- Play peek-a-boo
- Create a ritual that will work for just you and the baby. This is something that each parent can have separately with the baby.

As new parents, it is important to bring in a support system around the family. This can be in the form of either hospital staff in the beginning, parents, extended family, or friends. Taking care of a newborn becomes a full-time occupation at the beginning, therefore, a helping hand can only assist the parents in having enough time to spend with their baby.

Family and friends that you surround yourself with should be prepared to help you in any way that you would deem necessary such as through providing meals or helping to clean. Sometimes, it can even be in the form of babysitting at your home so that you can sneak a nap or a shower. Some babies are more demanding than others and taking small breaks such as these could also assist with developing a well-rounded bond.

A walk

Taking a walk with your baby can become a great bonding experience. Though the common belief is that babies should not leave the house for at least the first month of their life, that is a false claim. In fact, with the proper precautions, it is something that is encouraged as fresh air can be good for the baby, and the recovering mother.

The belief of not leaving the house started with the idea that babies do not have a developed immune system and parents should wait until at least the baby's first shots. However, this is one of the precautions that parents should take; to stay away from large crowds. Though it is impossible to completely make sure that a baby doesn't get sick, by staying away from large crowds it is something that parents can attempt to prevent.

Second, when going for a walk it is best to ensure that the baby is dressed for the appropriate weather. The rule of thumb would be that you should dress the baby the way that you dress yourself. For example, if you would dress yourself in layers, it is best to do that with the baby as well so that they do not get too cold or overheated.

Lastly, make sure that the baby is kept out of direct sunlight. Since babies cannot use sunblock for at least the first six months of their life, it is best to keep them in a shady area. If going for a walk with a stroller, this is usually pretty easy to do.

Bonding under unexpected circumstances

Try as we might, things rarely go according to plan. This is all the truer when it comes to the birth of a baby. No matter the best-laid birth plans that a mother carries to the hospital with her, babies follow what Mother Nature wants. In some instances, a baby may be born needing a little extra help, such as if they are born premature, and end up staying in the Neonatal Intensive Care Unit, or the NICU.

Parents dread hearing those four letters together: NICU. It always brings with it a connotation of fear and helplessness, however, that does not have to be the case. Whether the baby is brought back home right away or whether there is a NICU stay, it still requires the love of its parents to thrive and form a bond. This is a process that may be challenging at first, but plenty of hospital staff will be there to assist along the way.

A bond can be facilitated at the NICU by getting involved, much as in the case of a baby that has gone home. Though the involvement may be small, a parent should always ask to participate in any way that they are able to such as through diaper changes, bathing, or feeding. It has been proven that NICU babies thrive best in kangaroo care, which is where the baby is placed on the chest of a caregiver similar in fashion to the way a kangaroo holds their young.

When a baby is born, it automatically recognizes their mother through its various senses such as sense of smell, touch, and voice. Even if a baby is born premature, they are still able to make this recognition due to having spent its entire life up to that point inside of mom's belly.

Since the sense of smell is one of the most powerful senses and invokes memories, it can be used to help the baby not only form a bond, but also to help it grow and leave the NICU. It is suggested that a mom provide the baby with something that has their smell on. For example, some mothers will either provide a shirt they've been in, or they will sleep with a small piece of fabric that can be placed with the baby.

Talking with your baby is also very important at this stage. This type of bonding in the NICU can involve both parents as the baby has most likely heard dad before being born as well. This would be a good time to purchase baby books and begin reading those while spending time with the baby.

What may affect bonding

As important as bonding is, there are always those factors in life that will pose some sort of obstacle for the parents and the baby. Most of the factors mentioned are things that are beyond the control of the parents, and most likely, anyone else that is in the same situation.

For instance, perhaps the baby has shown up in the world looking much different than what was expected. This could be due to either the parents have formed some sort of perfect picture of their baby in their head, be it hair or eye color, or sometimes it could be because of a deformity. Though thorough screenings while pregnant can detect most abnormalities, there are those that still surprise the parents and medical staff. It is that surprising that could catch parents off guard making it difficult to move forward right away.

Hormones are raging the moment that a mother has given birth to her child, vaginally or through a c-section, there is no difference. Within the first few days after the birth of the baby, a mother can develop what is called the "baby blues". She may feel down, or weepy, for most of the time. Sometimes, it is also a combination of hormones and pure exhaustion having gone through hours of labor or the recovery of a c-section.

Postpartum depression, which women are now starting to discuss at length and openly, plays a very important role in being able to bond with the baby. A woman will never be able to tell ahead of time whether she will develop postpartum depression, however, if the "baby blues' do not start to go away within a couple of days from giving birth, it is important to reach out for help, even if it is to talk to a regular or the ob-gyn so that they may point you in the direction.

Most doctors now implement a questionnaire that is requested as they see both the mother and the baby, which means that you may end up encountering the same questionnaire multiple times at different doctors. It is important to be as forthcoming as possible so that if an intervention is needed, the help is provided as soon as is possible.

Common misconceptions

Even though it is proven that a baby needs to bond with its caregiver, the best of whom being mom and dad, there are always misleading schools of thought when it comes to how parents go about it. With new studies and advancements in medicine and science in general, various bonding methods have been proven to work. Unfortunately, there are still different misconceptions about the process which should be put to rest right here.

Bonding is instant

One of the most important pieces of information to remember when it comes to bonding with the baby is that it is not always instantaneous. The common belief is that parents love their baby immeasurably, from the moment that they are born; that they feel that bond right away. Nothing could be further from the truth. In fact, it is quite normal for any parent not to feel that overwhelming sense of rush they've been told happens from the moment they see their baby.

It is also a misconception that the baby itself will bond instantly. As a matter of fact, the reality is that babies do not necessarily care what is happening in the beginning so long as they are fed and allowed to sleep. It isn't until the baby is roughly two to three months will they develop a strong connection to a caregiver. This common misconception stems from observing other animals. For example, a duckling will imprint on the first thing that it sees and follows it around.

Even if that overwhelming feeling of love or bonding doesn't hit right away, that does not mean that it won't eventually happen. As mentioned, there are many ways in which the bond develops between the parents and baby, but it also takes time. Parents cannot get discouraged if they realize that they did not feel that bond right away. Instead, they should continue caring for their newborn as best as they can and allow the bond to form naturally over time. No matter how long it may take, caring for the newborn will facilitate the process.

Spoiled baby

Another common misconception when it comes to bonding is that the baby will end up spoiled. This belief is a result of the bonding instinct between the mother and baby that ensures that its needs are met. In order to effectively bond with the baby, it is recommended as much skin to skin time as is possible along with responding to your baby's cues without making them wait too long. This ensures that the baby understands that their needs will be met and that there are people who care about them. Since forming this bond requires the needs of the baby met to their fullest, an old-school mindset is that the baby will end up spoiled.

Now, no doubt there are kids that are actually spoiled out there, however, that is not as a result of bonding with the baby in the very beginning. A newborn cannot be spoiled because they do not yet understand the world the same way that older children do. They should not have to hear the word "no" or even understand its meaning since their needs are very basic. Denying a baby their basic needs that they are asking for, would not only break the bond that needs to form, but it may also irrevocably hurt the child in the long run.

Some of the most common types of myths out there are:

- Let the baby cry a little: the idea behind this is that a baby will cry to manipulate you, therefore, you should let them wait for a little before rushing to their aid to curb such tendencies. Though on average a newborn will cry roughly for three hours a day for at least the first three months of its life, it is not because she is trying to manipulate you. A baby at that age doesn't know how to manipulate yet, she is simply trying to communicate, and the only way in which she can do that is crying. This is the only way to say that she may be uncomfortable, tired, or hungry. It is best to always check, to the best of your ability, what the baby may need. Now, this is not to say that allowing them to cry for a moment will cause them undue harm, such as if there are other siblings involved that need to be taken care of. This is just to say that when possible, provide to the best of your ability so that the baby always knows that someone is there, helping them bond in the process.

- That the baby is being held too much: in fact, there is no such thing as holding your baby too much. As with preemies who respond well to kangaroo care, so it is also with full-term babies. With the development of various carriers and slings, it allows parents and babies to be close to one another. Contrary to what may be believed, especially with this myth, babies do not need their own alone, floor, or blanket time. By allowing the baby to feel secure with you, whether just through cuddling together, or wearing the baby and doing chores together, it helps the baby feel more secure when you are ready to place them on the floor for fun and learning.

- A routine is needed right away: in actuality, a routine isn't something that is needed until the baby is around three months in age, and even then, the routine should be focused mostly around nap times and bedtime. For the first three months, from the moment that the baby is born, the baby will be the one that dictates that routine or schedule of the day and that is how it should be. The baby will be the one that will determine what it needs and when and it is up to the parents to fulfill those needs, as they are very basic. Allowing the baby to connect and develop empathy is something that starts at the very beginning. Allowing the baby to choose the routine for that first couple of months will not spoil the baby in any way but will show it that it matters in this world and that people care.

Daycare ruins the bond

Some parents are in a situation where they need to start looking for daycare for their child right away, mostly due to the need to work. Essentially, living expenses have become so high that in many situations both parents have to work out of the house to provide enough income to live off of. There are many different types of daycare options out there, but most of them will require the baby to be dropped off with other caregivers for a good portion of the day.

The common misconception here is that if a baby is put into a daycare situation they will not spend enough time with their parents to be able to form that special bond. Studies have shown, however, that it is not the length of time that forms the bond, but the quality of the time that is spent together. The attachment that a baby is able to form with adoptive parents only helps to solidify the belief that it isn't about the length of time or genetics. It is always about what one does with that time that matters the most.

What this means for the parents is that when they are home with the baby in the morning, evenings, nights, and weekends, they focus solely on their baby and make the time meaningful. That is the time to put away the phone if feeding the baby and set aside the time to play together and make small routines.

Bonding in History

Most of the common misconceptions can actually be attributed to Marshall Klaus and John Kennell and their study of bonding and attachment that they performed in 1976. Though the study they performed used a very small sample of mothers and their newborns, they believed that they found the "critical period" of bonding. Specifically, they studied only 28 women who came from a low-income background. They believed based on their study that the best bonding time was the hour after the birth of the baby, much as is with animals.

Not long after, DeChateau, located out of Sweden, decided to study a small group of 62 middle-income mothers. Here, the findings specified that mothers who were allowed to spend more time with their children within 36 hours after their birth behaved much differently towards their newborns. They held their baby's more often, who in turn cried a lot less.

However, though DeChateau, as well as Klaus and Kennell, did show differences in bonding and mothers' actions as dependent upon how often they were able to spend time with their child, Svejda who studied 30 lower-middle-class mothers did not see any difference worth noting.

Though many tried to replicate the results of Klaus and Kennell, no one was able to do so, and it wasn't until 1984 that the two of them decided to re-evaluate what they found. They determined then, that there is not one process that leads to attachment or bonding.

Bonding was then concluded to have a much deeper meaning than anyone was able to study, the belief shifting to the idea that a bond starts forming when the baby is still in the womb. This is why it is said that biological parents can bond with their children, but adoptive parents need to develop an attachment outside of that bond.

Even though the findings were reviewed again and found inconclusive, the damage, as it were, had already been done. With their first findings out in the open, many people started to believe that bonding had to be instantaneous as opposed to something that could take an entire lifetime to make.

Bonding Cultural Beliefs

Cultural beliefs on bonding have a significant impact on how bonding takes place. Though in most cultures, the birth of a baby is seen as a joyful time, some cultures do not specifically facilitate the bond that needs to develop.

It was always the hunter and gatherer cultures that helped the bond to go due to the very nature of the society as a whole. In these cultures, the baby will spend most of its time with the mother as she works different chores. Most of the time, the baby will be on their mothers back and breastfeeding is encouraged right from the beginning.

In the western world, especially now, these types of cultural norms do not necessarily exist everywhere, and parents must work very hard for the bond that they seek. The western world prides itself on working and in some instances, families need both parents to work. This does not help mothers to bond with their children right from the get-go, with poor maternity plans in place or breastfeeding support which is no longer seen as the norm.

Indeed, the western world needs to work towards the goal of assisting parents in those crucial beginnings, especially when it comes to shifting their thoughts on breastfeeding children. With little to no support, especially outside of the home, mothers tend to give up this practice quite easily even if it was helping them bond with the baby they've known in the womb for nine months.

This cultural shift is beginning to take place, but it is very slow, which means that parents need to stand up to those norms that need to change. Mothers need to stand up for themselves and their right to breastfeed and have support in doing so.

Bonding with adoptive parents

By its very definition, bonding is something that can only happen between the birth parents and their child, but that does not mean anything bad for adoptive parents.

Adoptive parents get to go through a process that is called attachment. This is a two-way process, unlike bonding which is a one-way process, between the parents and the baby. Attachment tells the child that they matter to the parents, that they will always be there to protect it no matter what. In order for the family to grow with one another, this attachment must be achieved.

Parents can take some steps to ensure that the beginnings with the baby help this attachment to grow as it should:

- Feeding the baby: specifically, feeding the baby when she determined that she's hungry. Let the baby pick the schedule as it allows them to understand that their needs matter and you are willing to put them above your own.

- Eye contact: look into your baby's eyes often. Make contact while you are feeding the baby or playing together, as it facilitates the feeling of closeness. Let the baby look for you and come to you.

- Holding: and this could include anything from holding the baby, kissing, touching, cuddling, giving a small massage. The idea here is to show the baby as much affection as possible. Respond to the baby's cries as quickly as you can.

- Sound: which just means to talk to the baby, sing, read some books. Use a soft tone of voice and if you notice that other sounds startle your baby, try to minimize them until the baby gets accustomed.

- Playing together: though newborns sleep most of the day, play with them as much as possible such as through peek-a-boo.

Attachment is as important to develop for adoptive parents as bonding is for natural parents. An attachment bond takes a little bit more work on both the parents and the baby, but it can be just as meaning as a bond is. Much like any other parent, adoptive parents will also go through their own emotional struggles and must keep this attachment in perspective.

As much as any parent would like everything to go as smoothly as possible, that is rarely the case. Parents must not get discouraged as the beginnings with a newborn are usually a trying time. Babies, whether adopted or not, will naturally cry for various reasons, but it is how parents react to those cries that will determine the type of bond or attachment that will develop.

One very important thing to remember is that as an adoptive parent, you are not alone. Many parents who adopt their children go through the same processes and worry about mostly the same things. If you find yourself worrying about any part of the process, it is best to reach out to support groups or other parents because at the very least it'll be easier to see that this journey is not a solitary one.

Takeaway

Bonding is a process that, though it is natural, is not always something that is instant. Parents that adopt a child have just as much of a chance of bonding with the baby as parents who have had their own baby. Sometimes, bonding is difficult for different reasons, but parents should not give up right away. It is the hard work that is given to the child that builds that bond all parents hope for.

Attachment, much like bonding, is a process that is not always instant, but it is something that is very important for the family to grow together. It is up to the parents to help facilitate a good environment for the attachment to grow, understanding that it will involve hard work, which will be greatly rewarded.

Not all cultures are alike and in some culture the bond is not something that society as a whole bother themselves with. These are the cultural norms that need to be taken down by parents to ensure that each and every generation has the ability to grow into the best people that they can be.

Take the time to make those small bonding or attachment moments mentioned above and take the time for you. Any parent that has asked for help and has rested themselves, is better able to continue caring for their baby in a way that will help the bond or attachment to thrive.

CHAPTER 2:

Feeding a Newborn

Feeding a newborn baby can be quite daunting for some first-time parents. Those feelings are normal to have in the beginning and they can be overcome with practice and patience. When it comes to feeding a baby, there is no one correct way to do it, however, there are guidelines. These guidelines provide safe practices that will work to point new parents in the best direction for their family.

From the moment that a baby is born, there are two options for feeding which include breastfeeding or formula feeding. Feeding any type of solids won't start until the fourth month at the very earliest, and even then, the baby has to meet certain milestones before trying any type of solids. Though parents always look forward to this milestone, it is not one that should be hurried. Most of the time, the baby will let parents know when they are ready to move on to the next stages of feeding.

Below is an outline of breastfeeding and formula feeding so that parents can make the decision that will work best for them. As with many things, the decision is completely up to the parents and there is no right or wrong answer. Every avenue has its benefits and its downfalls, and all must be evaluated for the best answer. As this topic can be a rather controversial one, it is best to not allow anyone to sway your decision, but rather do what is best for you and your family.

Breastfeeding

The American Academy of Pediatrics as well as the American College of Obstetricians and Gynecologists strongly suggest that a baby be strictly breastfed for the first six months of its life. Their suggestion means that a baby would strictly receive breastmilk, whether straight from the breast or through a bottle, without receiving anything else such as formula, water, or juice.

Though the AAP make breastmilk the recommended source of nourishment for babies, undertaking breastfeeding is a very personal decision. Breast-feeding comes with as many challenges as it does rewards and should be carefully considered. Most people have strong opinions about breastfeeding whether they support it or not, making that something that has to be contended with.

No matter the opinion of the public, breastmilk is a wonderful source of nutrients for the baby. Breastmilk has the perfect balance of all vitamins, proteins, and fats that the baby will require for those first six crucial months of its life. Though breastmilk is forever being studied, it was determined that it is able to adjust itself to what the baby needs at any given time. For example, breastmilk can provide the baby with specific antibodies if the baby starts feeling under the weather. The information for what the baby needs is passed down to the mother through the baby's saliva as it feeds directly from the breast.

In that fashion, breastmilk regulates its supply based on how much and how often the baby eats. Most advocate for breastfeeding on demand which means allowing the baby to sit on the breast however long it wants whenever the baby demands it. Some mothers breastfeed on a schedule, where the baby has put to the breast every three to four hours and nurses for a set amount of time, usually at fifteen minutes on each side.

The method in which the baby is fed will depend, most of the time, on the baby itself. Some babies will adapt a schedule all on their own, and some will demand food more often. One point to remember is that the baby must be fed at night as well until the pediatrician has deemed that the baby gained enough weight. Until the baby at least doubles in weight from their birth weight, they must be woken in the middle of the night, or dream fed at least every three to four hours. This will ensure that the baby stays fed and hydrated allowing them to gain the right amount of weight.

Breastfeeding obstacles

The journey of breastfeeding starts right after the baby's birth with the assistance of a nurse, lactation consultant, or a midwife. No matter how the baby enters the world, whether at the hospital, c-section or at home with a midwife, that journey can begin. In most instances, the baby will be put to the breast as soon as the mother is able to hold her baby and take instruction.

It is important to ask as many questions as you can and accept the help that is given while embarking on this journey. As with many things, there may be some obstacles, but they can be overcome if the mother would like to continue with that journey. Some of the most common obstacles and what can be done about them are:

- Pain! Breastfeeding can be a painful process in the beginning as the nipples begin getting used to the baby eating every couple of hours if not sooner. Some homemade remedies can be tried such as soothing the nipples with nipple cream, checking the baby's latch, and air-drying your nipples. Placing some breastmilk on them could also assist them in healing quicker. In a case where the pain does not start to subside, the mother should reach out for additional assistance such as by contacting a lactation consultant.

- The mother doesn't produce enough breastmilk. At first, the breasts provide a liquid called colostrum which is the most beneficial to the baby by providing it with fat-rich nutrients and immune-boosting antibodies. Since a newborn baby's stomach capacity is no more than the size of a cherry, the baby does not need to consume large amounts of it. Within a couple of days, breastmilk comes in and begins to regulate itself based on the baby's demands. When demand changes so does the mother's supply, however, a fussy baby does not automatically mean that there is not enough supply. As the baby grows it goes through various growth spurts which cause the baby to eat more and more often. It is quite alright to allow the baby to do so without further interfering so long as the baby is still producing enough urine and stools. Studies show that those are the times when women usually stop breastfeeding as they are unaware of the process, whereas they should continue through those harder times. The time to consult a medical professional starts the moment that the baby is no longer gaining weight or producing enough diapers as you do not want the baby to get dehydrated.

- Your baby has the wrong latch. The baby can have an incorrect latch for various reasons such as the mother having inverted or flat nipples, the baby was premature, or the baby has a tongue or lip tie. If the issue is inverted or flat nipples and the baby is unable to grab a good hold of them, there are nipples shields that can be purchased at most drug stores that assist the baby by bringing the nipple to the front. In other cases, a medical professional can be asked to provide assistance by showing either different breastfeeding positions or determining if the baby may need to have a tongue or lip tie resolved. Most babies are able to continue breastfeeding after a lip and tongue procedure without any problems.

- A mother's breasts are leaky or hard. In those cases, not only does breastfeeding become a chore, but it can be painful even if the baby has the proper latch. Great care must be taken to allow the baby to continue latching, but also to prevent inflammation of the breasts cause mastitis which is very painful and can cause infection. In the case of hard and full breasts the baby must be fed more often, or the milk expressed so that it does not build up to cause the inflammation. If a baby is having a hard time latching in that situation, a little milk can be expressed by the mother first to make the latching easier for the baby.

- The mother may miss her body belonging to just her. Breastfeeding a child means that some guidelines still have to be adhered to, much as they did during pregnancy. Though they are not as strict, in some instances it is true that what mom eats so does the baby. That is why it is advised that mothers try and refrain from drinking too much alcohol or caffeine and still stay away from certain foods. After nine months of pregnancy, it is difficult for a mother to imagine having to go through certain restraints again for at least another six months to a year, and those thoughts are quite normal to have.

Benefits of Breastfeeding

Breastfeeding comes with as many benefits as it does obstacles. Even if a baby is not breastfed for a full year, since a baby still requires either breastmilk or formula after six months of life, both mother and baby can still reap the rewards of providing breastmilk.

- Breastfeeding has been known to lower the risk of SIDS (Sudden Infant Death Syndrome). Scientists have not been able to secure an answer as to why that is, but studies have shown that fewer babies suffer from SIDS when they are breastfed.

- As mentioned earlier, it allows the bond between mother and baby to form and to stay secure.

- Breastmilk protects the baby against many different diseases such as Type 1 Diabetes and spinal meningitis.

- It has been linked to smarter babies which have been tested through IQ scores later on in life.

- Breastfeeding mitigates the possibility of obesity as the baby gains weight at just the right amount.

- For mothers, there is a benefit of burning extra calories as well as assisting in the contracting of the uterus back to its pre-pregnancy size.

Though there are wonderful benefits to breastfeeding a baby, in some instances that is not an option. Anyone of the obstacles mentioned can hinder a mother's ability to provide breastfeed exclusively, but there is still the option of pumping breastmilk if there is breastmilk available. Of course, this option would not work if the mother was having a hard time actually getting a supply of breastmilk no matter the steps that she chose to do so.

Many mothers choose the route of pumping breastmilk whether they return to work or not, either because they have had trouble breastfeeding (such as the wrong latch), or for personal reasons such as wanting others to be able to care for the baby as well and having the freedom to step away.

Pumping is a good way to build up a stash of frozen breastmilk that can be used later down the road.

Pumping

Mothers also choose to breast pump if they have to go back to work before the baby is eating regular food. In the United States, the law requires that employers provide a new mother with an appropriate place and ample time to pump milk during the day. It is recommended that a mother pumps every few hours, most choose between three and four hours, to ensure that supply does not dwindle.

When proceeding with pumping, whether exclusively or just at work, the mother can purchase a pump through her health insurance plan if she has one. It should be mentioned that the flanges which attach to the breast are not a one size fit all. Nipples come in all different sizes; therefore, the flanges should be measured to ensure a correct fit. If the flange is the wrong size, it may not suction correctly and either cause pain to the nipple or not stimulate the nipple enough to produce enough of a supply of milk.

Since pumped breastmilk is going to be stored outside of the body, there are some steps that need to be taken to ensure that it is still being provided as fresh as possible.

- Freshly Expressed breastmilk: this is milk that has just been expressed by hand or pump straight into a bottle. It can last on the countertop, at regular room temperature for up to four hours. If it is refrigerated, it can last up to 4 days, so long as the refrigerator is properly cooling. In a freezer, it can last up to 6 months. Though it can be used up to 12 months if it is in a deep freezer, it is best to use it as quickly as possible.

- Thawed milk that was previously frozen: once it is defrosted, it can last up to two hours on a countertop at normal room temperature. Once defrosted, but not brought completely to warmth, it can stand in the refrigerator for up to one day. To ensure that bacteria are not introduced, it can never be refrozen.

- Milk leftover in a bottle from a feeding: it needs to be used within two hours after the baby last ate the bottle. This means that milk that has been defrosted or freshly expressed, cannot be refrigerated or frozen once the baby has started eating from that bottle even if they do not finish it.

Breastmilk is hard to come by, a woman who has decided to pump can only attest to the hard work that goes into being able to express it and freeze it for later. For this simple fact, it is best to start with a smaller amount until the baby shows the desire to continue eating, as opposed to making a very large bottle where most of it will end up going to waste.

Formula

Infant formula has a long history that dates back to the 19th century. In 1865, a chemist named Justus von Liebig is the first to develop and patent commercially available infant formula. It did not become popular until 1958 when it became more accessible to the common mother causing breastfeeding to go out of favor. Since then, the question of whether to breastfeed or use infant formula has been a controversial debate among mothers.

Ultimately, the choice on whether to use infant formula rests solely with the parents of the child and is the best substitute to breastmilk. There are many reasons why parents would decide to use formula instead of breastfeeding, but the reason for its use should not matter to anyone else. Much as with breastfeeding, there are pros and cons with the use of infant formula and barring a situation where infant formula is the only answer, those pros and cons should be considered.

Formula obstacles

As breastfeeding comes with its own set of obstacles, so does infant formula.

- Formula and all the accessories needed can be expensive. Since the baby will be eating multiple times throughout the day, that will require many bottles to be purchased ahead of time. On average, the cost of formula is around $0.19 for an ounce which means that for a year of formula the cost will be around $1,700. Parents must also add the aforementioned costs such as bottles and nipples.

- Infant formula must be prepared each time to ensure that it is measured correctly and to the appropriate temperature. This will cause some distress as the baby will likely expect the food to be provided right away. The formula cannot be prepared too hot or, in some instances, too cold due to the baby's preference.

- The formula is harder to digest than breastmilk which means that it is possible for the baby to become constipated and gassy. In the beginning, it is also possible that some cans of formula will end up going to waste due to such issues as parents have to try multiple different formulas in order to find one that fits their baby best.

- Lastly, the formula doesn't have the same protective properties that breastmilk does. Since breastmilk is tailored to each baby specifically, and colostrum is so full of antibodies, it is not something that infant formula would ever be able to provide.

Benefits of Infant Formula

Using infant formula does also come with its benefits even if they are different from the benefits that breastfeeding provides.

- Mother is able to get a break when needed, or even something as simple as being able to run to the store alone, since a family member or caretaker is able to feed the baby as well.

- With infant formula, it is easier to see how much the baby is eating. This can alleviate a lot of stress that breastfeeding mothers get because they are not sure if the baby is getting enough or gaining enough weight.

- Since all infant formula is regulated to provide the baby with the same benefits, what mother eats doesn't bother the baby. With breastmilk, the mother's diet will affect what the baby eats, therefore, she would need to abstain from things such as alcohol or excessive amounts of caffeine. A mother using infant formula does not have that to worry about.

- Babies that are fed using formula do not need to eat as often as babies that are breastfed. This means, that they do not have to be fed in the middle of the night quite as often or for as long as breastfed babies do. This provides the mother and the baby with more restful sleep.

As with breastmilk, there are certain guidelines when it comes to the making and storage of formula bottles. They must be adhered to as much as possible to mitigate the possibility of any bacteria being introduced.

- Once a container of powder formula has been opened it must be stored in the sealed container (best to use the same one that it comes in) in a dry place to prevent molding.

- The unmixed formula, such as the powder formula, should not be stored in the refrigerator, but rather at room temperature.

- It is best that the powder formula is used within one month of being opened.

- It is possible to make bottles of formula ahead of time as long as they are kept within the refrigerator. Some parents decide to make enough formula to last twenty-four hours, the longest length of time suggested in the guidelines before it needs to be thrown away, by storing formula in a large container in the refrigerator. You can also make one bottle ahead of time so that all you have to worry about is warming up the bottle itself.

- Any prepared or ready-to-feed formula needs to be thrown out within one hour if it has been sitting untouched.

- Any formula, whether prepared or ready-to-feed, needs to be discarded if the baby is not showing any interest in the remaining portion. This will prevent any bacteria from being introduced to the baby.

The formula has had its ups and downs since its invention. With each decade the trend on what was best, whether formula or the breast, changed. At one time, formula was seen as the "rich" way to do it, due to the sheer cost of it all. It still remains a rather costly thing, but it is no longer seen as something that those that are considered rich have to do to show their status.

Burping

With feeding comes the wonderful task of burping the baby, a task which many parents fail to do properly. When a baby has not been burped properly, or for the best amount of time, unintended consequences tend to happen.

Most of the time, parents will lay the baby back down much sooner than they should have. This causes the baby to start to spit up or gas. This causes the baby to lose the precious milk or formula that they've been given, starting the process over again. In some instances, the baby will actually wake up screaming because they are in pain from the trapped gas.

Burping is an essential part of the feeding process, no matter how long it might take. Some babies are great at being burped, whereas some babies will require a little more work. Therefore, different burping techniques have been developed to aid parents in deciding which one works best for their baby.

- Over-the-shoulder: this is one of the most common burping techniques. As the name suggests, you put the baby high on your chest with the baby's chin resting on your shoulder. From there, you pat or rub the baby's back gently until they burp.

- Face-down: in this technique, you place the baby face down across your lap, and as above, you gently put or rub their back. You have to make sure that the baby's head is supported on your lap and facing one side so as not to cause any undue harm or possible spit up before the baby has a chance to actually burp.

- Baby exercises: this technique involves a series of different exercises that can be done with the baby that encourage burping. These include leg bicycles or moving legs up and down and in a circular motion.

- Upright: here the baby is sat upright on your lap facing one side. With one hand you would support the baby's head and with the other gently pat or rub their back until they burp.

These are by no means a one-size fit type deal and as parents, you would need to figure out what works best for your baby. Remember, each baby is different and will respond differently to every technique.

Though it may add a couple of more minutes to a feeding session, which at night might feel like forever, it is time well spent. It will ensure that the baby can remain happy for a longer period of time, and in the night or nap time, make sure that they are not woken up too early because of gas pains that could have been avoided.

Necessary Accessories

Whether as a family you choose to breastfeed or formula feed the baby, there are certain things that will need to be obtained in order to make feeding not just successful, but also something that can be enjoyed.

Breast Pump

Even if the choice has been made to exclusively breastfeed the baby, which means not supplementing with any formula, a breast pump should be either purchased or obtained through the insurance provider. It is now the law in the U.S. that any health insurance that is covering the woman during her pregnancy, has to provide her with a breast pump. Every insurance has its own rulers on how they cover the machine, for example, some will only send it thirty days before the due date, therefore, it is best to contact them for further information.

There are different types of breast pumps out there, and the choice on which to use will be based on the overall need. If a mother is exclusively breastfeeding and staying at home with the baby, she may not need a large and powerful breast pump just to store a couple of ounces of milk in the freezer, but a woman who is working outside the home may need something more powerful.

- Manual pumps: these pumps are operated by hand and work either with the squeeze of a trigger or through sliding a cylinder back and forth. They are usually small, rather inexpensive, and can be purchased at most stores. They are great for convenience, but they will not work well if the mother needs to express large amounts of milk. Not only would that get time-consuming, but it can also become tiring.

- Battery operated: pumps such as these can become a great alternative to the manual breast pump, but still only work best if there is not a large need for pumping more than once a day. Much as the manual pump, it is convenient, but it can become more costly because of the need to keep replacing its batteries. This is the reason that it is recommended only if pumping is restricted to once a day at most.

- Electric pumps: are more powerful and will yield the best results. Electric pumps are recommended for mothers who want to pump more than once a day, either to make a stash because they overproduce or want some milk stored for a rainy day, mothers that work and find themselves in need of pumping while out of the house, or of course, the mother who pumps exclusively for various reasons. They are more expensive than the previous two options, but they may be covered with insurance as mentioned earlier.

Some mothers also look into purchasing second-hand pumps to cut down on the cost, or to have a spare. A spare can come in handy if the mother goes to work daily, or almost daily, and does not want to carry the pump back and forth between home and work as it can become a burden. Before making such a person, it is best to keep in mind that anything that comes in to contact with breastmilk will need to be replaced.

Due to this, it is best to avoid purchasing a manual or battery-operated pumps second-hand, however, since they are run relatively inexpensive, it should not be too troublesome to purchase them new. On the other hand, most brands of electric pumps have parts that can be replaced rather cheaply and the pump itself that never comes in to contact with breastmilk can be sterilized.

Keep in mind that the accessories that come with a pump, even if it is new, need to be replaced from time to time. The manual that is provided with your particular pump will point you in the right direction on when to replace certain parts and where they can be purchased. Though most of those items are inexpensive, especially as compared to purchasing the formula in the long run, it is always best to shop around for the best price as some items do not necessarily have to be name brand.

If a breast pump is obtained, and all the parts for it, you will also need to purchase milk storage bags. There are many options out there as many baby-oriented companies have made their own variations, but they all work mostly the same. There are also bottles designed for milk storage in the freezer, but they do take up more space, therefore, if you do not have a stand-alone freezer you will be using, it is best to purchase bags that can be easily flattened and kept in the freezer in a storage bin or box.

Bottles

No matter the way in which the baby will be primarily fed, it is best to purchase at least some bottles. There will be a need for anywhere between four and ten bottles, depending on how the baby is fed. For a baby that is exclusively breastfeeding and may take a bottle only on occasion, you may not need any more than four bottles. However, for a baby that is fed primarily using formula, it is best to have closer to ten.

A baby will eat at least every three to four hours, therefore, the more bottles that are on hand, the less washing that has to be done. In the beginning, bottles have to be sterilized to ensure that as much bacteria as possible is neutralized. The process of sterilization will go on for some time, most of the time until the baby is at least six months of age and its immune system has started to develop.

Nowadays, there are many different types of bottles on the market. There are bottles made of glass and others of plastic. Some are regular bottles with a nipple and a cover, and some have special inserts in order to become anti-colic. If making the purchase of bottles before the baby is born, it is best to purchase the minimum and if at all possible, at least one of each type. This way, if the baby doesn't take to one type of bottle, a lot of money has not been wasted.

Bottle warmer

Though a bottle warmer is not always a necessary item, it is one that becomes quite handy in the long run. A baby's bottle, whether it provides formula or breastmilk, cannot be made too warm. In some instances, a baby will also not take a bottle that is too cold just because of personal preference.

Using the microwave is not something that is highly advised for either breastmilk or formula. First and foremost, microwaving breastmilk will reduce the number of nutrients that are found within and which the baby sorely needs. Secondly, whether it is breastmilk or formula, a microwave causes hot pockets of liquid to form within the bottle instead of uniformly warming it up. This may cause the baby to be burned while they are drinking the milk.

A bottle warmer is the easiest way to warm a bottle to the precise temperature that would be good for the baby. Most of these warmers use steam to warm the bottle whether it is frozen breastmilk or formula in need of warming.

As mentioned, this is not a strictly necessary item, however, it does make things a little easier. Without a bottle warmer it is necessary to find other ways in which to warm a bottle such as thawing frozen breastmilk and warming the bottle on the stove. The same would go for formula since it is usually mixed with cold water. If you feel that the stove may be an easier alternative, the bottle warmer can be skipped altogether. It is also an item that can be purchased later once you realize you may actually prefer that method to the stove.

Nursing pillow

Many breastfeeding mothers choose to purchase a breastfeeding pillow. Usually, this type of pillow is in a "C" shape and will sit comfortably around the mother's midsection. A good and supportive nursing pillow will actually assist the baby to get a good latch. It also has been known to help the mother by taking the strain off the arms and back or shoulders by having to hold the baby in the right position. The pillow will actually bring the baby to the perfect height for feeding.

Some mothers who do not breastfeed also choose to use such a pillow as it helps hold the baby in the right position to take a bottle, easing the strain on the hand and back.

A nursing pillow, such as a Boppy, is also used to help the baby do "tummy time". Once the baby is a little older and is curiously looking around, one of these pillows can be placed on a floor with the baby on its stomach to help them lift their heads and explore their surroundings making such a pillow useful in the long run besides just feeding.

To Go Items

Unless you plan on becoming a hermit, it is best to take the baby outside even for smaller walks around the park. Until the baby is able to sit at a table and eat what the parents eat, which may be some time, it is best to bring along a few things that may assist in feeding the baby outside the home.

- Nursing cover; If you are breastfeeding your baby and are not comfortable on the outside, it is best to bring a nursing cover. There are also covers out there that have multiple uses, so you are not just bringing along one extra thing. Some will actually work to cover the infant car seat part of a stroller, allowing the baby to go for a ride in peace without prying outside of the outside world.

- Bottle cooler: this can be used both by mothers who breastfeed and formula feed. Some mothers are not comfortable breastfeeding outside the home and choose to bring bottled breastmilk instead. Whichever you choose to use to feed your baby, a cooler for bottles can become handy as a way to store them. Remember, breastmilk does not have to be cooled for at least a couple of hours if it is fresh, but if you are going to be outside longer it may be best to bring an insulated cooler. This could work for formula as well as some parents choose to take with them prefilled bottles of water. An insulated cooler could actually keep the bottles warmer to the temperature that the baby will be comfortable drinking.

- Formula dispenser: as the name specifies, this is for formula-fed babies, though some parents use these for snacks later as well. These dispensers usually have a couple of compartments where you can prefill specific amounts of formula to fill with water later. Though this can be substituted with small baggies, it makes pouring the formula into the bottle without a scooper that much easier. They are also not that expensive so as to break the bank.

These are just some small suggestions to help make a trip out of the house easier. When leaving home with a baby plenty already has to get packed and having a small list handy is a good idea. That way, you do not find yourself running around to a store trying to find formula because you may not have grabbed any.

Takeaway

How to feed a newborn is a decision that the parents have to come into agreement on, as breastfeeding requires a lot of support. Parents also have to be prepared that sometimes even the best-laid plans don't go accordingly. When it comes to feeding that happens quite often and there is nothing wrong with changing your mind to something else that would work for the family.

If breastfeeding is just not the ideal choice, the formula has been developed as the most practical and best alternative which offers more or less the same nutrients that breastmilk would. Though there is a bigger push for breastfeeding nowadays for breastfeeding, it by no means signifies that parents are doing anything incorrectly if they choose to either start with or move on to using formula instead.

As with many things in life, there will be those that discuss the merits of one over the other and not necessarily in the privacy of their own home. Parents need not worry about what others think and instead focus on ensuring that their baby is fed, no matter which way that may be. Fed is best, as they now say, and that is just how as it should be. Sooner or later, all babies will start to eat solids, making the whole discussion of breast vs formula a moot point. As long as all babies are allowed to thrive up until that moment is all that matters in the long run.

CHAPTER 3:

Newborn Sleep

The sleep of a newborn is the most elusive thing that there is. It is one of the things that concerns parents the most, mostly because they would like to sleep, exhausted as they are from taking care of a newborn baby. It is fretted about by sleep-deprived caretakers straight from the beginning, especially since newborns do not sleep a lot by their very nature of being newborns. On average, in the first year, parents lose around fifty hours of precious sleep, which is why this topic is such a tense one and parents will do anything for a wink of sleep.

What's most important to remember here, before getting started, is that every newborn is different in their own way. Some sleep better than others and it does not do well for anyone to compare one baby to another. Even among siblings, the changes in sleep patterns can be quite drastic and, unfortunately for the parents, there is no one right answer to what would make a baby sleep better.

Some guidelines can be provided that will assist you, as the parent, in making the best decisions for your family, from safe sleep practices, to where babies can sleep, and if a schedule is at all a feasible option for a newborn, or whether that is something that will have to wait.

General Sleep Information

Generally speaking, a newborn will sleep most of the day, somewhere between 14 and 17 hours in 24 hours, waking only for a diaper change and feeding. Some babies may even sleep as much as 18 or 19 hours. Since babies have small stomachs and are still getting used to the outside world, they don't sleep for long periods of time.

Breastfed babies tend to wake quicker, somewhere around two to three hours, whereas babies that are formula-fed wake somewhere between three and four hours. It should also be mentioned that in the first few weeks of life, babies should be fed at the same intervals throughout the night even if the baby is showing signs of sleeping longer. This is important to ensure that the baby gains the proper amount of weight within the first few weeks of life. A pediatrician would best be able to advise on when the baby no longer needs to be fed during the night if they continue sleeping longer.

Same as adults, babies have different stages of sleep: REM, or rapid eye movement, and non-REM sleep. REM sleep is the lighter of the two, where dreaming and eye movement occurs. Even though babies sleep for most of the day in the beginning, at least half of their sleep time is actually spent in REM sleep.

Non-REM sleep has four stages for both adults and babies, and they are listed below:

1. This is the initial stage where most of the dozing off happens. Eyes get droopy and tend to open and close.

2. Sleep is still light at this stage and the baby is easy to startle.

3. A deep sleep where the baby is quiet and does not move.

4. In this stage, sleep is very deep, and the baby won't move at all.

It is in those moments that parents question whether they will ever sleep again. The simple answer is that yes, sleep will finally come! Even if the baby takes longer than parents would like, they will eventually sleep for longer intervals. In the meantime, it is best to review some of the tips presented here.

Safe Sleep

Guidelines

With as much as babies sleep, it is the parents' obligation to ensure that the baby sleeps is in a safe environment to minimize the risk of SIDS. Safe sleep is of the utmost importance as on average, there are around 3,500 sleep-related deaths in the U.S. alone.

When it comes to safe sleep, there are four basic things to remember:

1. The baby needs to sleep on his back. This is a recommendation until the baby is at least one year of age at which point they should be mobile enough on their own to change positions without getting hurt. The baby should be dressed in pajamas that do not have any loose pieces and will not cover the baby's head. Until the baby is able to roll on their own, they can be swaddled to ensure that they are kept warm, but not overheated. There are plenty of different swaddles on the market, however, the rule of thumb is to ensure that the baby's face will not be covered, and they will not be able to roll in their sleep in it. If a baby isn't swaddled and starts to roll over on to their side or stomach, it is perfectly all right to move the baby back on to their back while

they sleep. In 2015, the CDC performed a study and found that one in every five mothers report that they put their baby to sleep either on its stomach or side, as is not advised.

2. The baby requires a firm sleep surface. This could consist of a firm mattress that is placed inside a safety-approved crib or a bassinet designed for overnight sleep. A baby should never be placed anywhere that is soft or in a crib with bumpers attached. Soft mattresses and bumpers proved to be a suffocation hazard as a baby can unknowingly press their nose into the bedding without being able to move themselves back into the correct sleeping position.

3. Any soft bedding such as blankets, pillows, or comforters should be removed. Much as a soft mattress or crib bumpers, any loose items around the crib like blankets and pillows are a suffocation hazard to the baby. In the beginning, the baby will not have the ability to move things away from their face should it get covered. If the baby has something within their reach, they are liable to pull it towards themselves without being able to free their nose or mouth. To put it into perspective, the CDC has found that around 39% of mothers state they use some sort of soft bedding in their baby's sleep space even though it has been deemed an unsafe practice.

4. Baby should share the parents' bedroom, but not their actual bed. Though companies have designed ways for the baby to join their parents in bed, it is still safest to have the baby in their own space. If parents are not comfortable putting the baby into their own crib until the baby is older, there are regular and bed-side bassinets that can be purchased. They are smaller than a full crib and can be easily reached in the middle of the night. In this fashion, the baby has their own space preventing any possibility of suffocation due to either the parents rolling on to the baby inadvertently or covering the baby with either comforters or pillows.

Safe Space

Along with safe sleep comes the choice of where the baby should sleep as parents do have a couple of options. The key is to ensure that the baby will stay safe during the night and be comfortable.

- The crib: is the most common choice by parents, not just in the U.S., but all over the world. There are many different options and looks such as metal or wooden, black or white. The size of a crib is perfect for a nursery or bedroom but will allow the baby to use it for some time. The crib is designed in a way that allows the mattress to be lowered, but because of the bars that make up the crib stops the baby from rolling out. It is, however, not a portable option at all and does take up quite a bit of space if living conditions are tight.

- Bassinet: this is a much smaller version of a crib, which can only be used for a baby that has not rolled over or sat up yet. It is much more portable and can be moved from room to room or to another house if need be but cannot be used for as long as a crib and another option will need to be found once the baby outgrows this. To some parents, this is an unnecessary expense.

- A cradle: this sleep space is even smaller than a bassinet but has the added option of a rocking motion. Since they are smaller than a crib and bassinet, they too are very portable and help with putting the baby to sleep, but the baby will outgrow this option in a blink of an eye.

- Co-Sleeper: a great option for parents who would like to co-sleep but minimize the risk of SIDS or asphyxiation. A co-sleeper is designed to mimic a bassinet where one of the sides gets removed and placed along the side of the bed. This provides easy access to the newborn and is even encouraged for breastfeeding mothers. Of course, like a bassinet, the co-sleeper will become too small for the baby in a very short amount of time.

- The play yard or pack-and-play: is a very popular option especially for parents that are on a budget. They are roughly the size of a crib but can be broken down and made portable. Most of them are on at least two wheels, which makes it easier to bring from one room to another. Since they are almost the same size as a crib, with a mattress that is low to the ground, it can be used for a longer period of time than a bassinet, but still not as long as a crib. There is the chance that by the time the baby outgrows this option, they can be moved into a regular toddler bed.

- Baby swing: though many parents swear by having a sling for their child, this is an item that requires a lot of research. Each brand and type of swing has its own specifications, and some are not recommended for newborns. Most are not recommended for sleep, especially through the night, therefore, though it might be a great item to have in order to be able to place the baby somewhere, it is not something that would be recommended for sleep through the night.

Scientific studies have determined the best ways for a baby to be placed down for sleep whether it is for a nap or bedtime. The rule of thumb is to ensure that the baby is always placed on its back, until it can turn on its own, and does not have anything loose around it such as comforters or blankets. There are many options out there for where to put the baby down to sleep, which will not necessarily all work for each family. Based on the information presented above, it is best to continue doing research to determine what works best for your family.

It is understandable that not all families would like to use a crib, which makes bassinets a better option. For parents who would like their baby close and like the idea of sharing a space, the co-sleeper becomes a great solution. Funds also play a big role in what you would choose for your family. If you have a bit more to work with, or you know someone could assist such as by purchasing a gift at a baby shower, you can use both the bassinet and crib. If you want one stable place a baby can use for a while, maybe a crib that converts into a toddler bed is the best answer.

Whichever you choose to work with, you just have to remember the safe sleep practices and do further research on the item you intend to obtain. Some items such as cribs or pack-and-plays have expiration dates where they are only certified as safe until that day has passed, same as car seats. As mentioned, some swings cannot be used with babies until they reach a certain weight or height requirement, therefore, it is best to ensure you know exactly what you are purchasing and that your baby will be safe.

...ting Baby on Schedule

The idea of a schedule is one that is debated amongst parents, however, in the beginning, it is the baby that will end up setting the schedule throughout the day. Most of the time, that schedule will be eating, sleep, then poop over and over again, in roughly two to four-hour intervals. Plenty of times, however, babies confuse their day and night with one another. It is in those times that attempting to set some sort of schedule that could be continued as the baby grows, is of vital importance.

Within the first two weeks of the baby's life, a routine isn't the most important part so much as allowing the baby to understand the difference between day and night. As mentioned, babies tend to confuse the two, therefore, it is up to the parents to help the baby distinguish. This can be done simply by making small routines around different times of the day. Those small routines are the ones that will help the baby make the connection between what is night and what is the day.

A possible day time routine:

- Opening up the blinds
- Turning on as many lights as needed
- Allowing for ample noise
- Small amounts of playtime during awake time

- Rousing the baby fully before feeding
- Do not allow for stretches of sleep that are too long, meaning to still feed the baby within two to three hours so the longer stretches happen at night.

A possible nighttime routine:

- Quieting the house
- Closing the blinds and turning down any bright lights
- A small bedtime routine to consist of a bath, book reading, and snuggle time
- Avoiding any stimulating activity
- Feed the baby when they wake, but avoid turning on any bright lights

When the baby is roughly a month old, it is best to start implementing a routine that will revolve around times of the day. Most of the same suggestions from above can be kept within this routine, but now implementing an actual bedtime will benefit both the baby and the parents in the long run. There is really no set time in which things should happen as each family and its needs are different, therefore, there is no one right answer. It is best to evaluate possible bedtimes or nap times as they would coincide with the parents already existing obligations such as work or school.

What should be avoided at such a young age is sleep training your baby. A newborn is not yet old enough to understand sleep patterns and has not taught themselves how to self-sooth. Parents must first teach the baby how to self-soothe before they can try and sleep train a baby a couple of months down the road.

The idea is to lay down the foundations in the very beginning for good sleep later on. There is technically nothing getting in the parents' way of teaching their baby how to sleep through the night by around three months of age, though parents do have to also understand that this process may take a little longer than is desired.

Sleep Problems

Most parents want to know the signs of sleep problems and what to do about them, however, what parents usually assume is a problem is generally a normal part of infant sleep patterns. Some of the most common patterns that parents assume are issues include:

1. The baby waking more at night, whether they slept through the night or not. Though this may prove problematic, especially for the parents who will start to lack sleep throughout that time, this is quite normal. Usually, this happens around the time a baby is going through a growth spurt and require more food to grow. The baby with a newborn, there is no real solution to this as the baby does need more

64

food. In some instances, it could be solved by providing nourishment that will sustain the baby longer, such as supplementing with formula or talking to the pediatrician about other options.

2. The baby needing someone to be present when they fall asleep. This could mean that the baby requires to be rocked to sleep or the parent sitting next to them. Again, this is a normal phenomenon. For nine months, or around there, the baby has been inside of mom, kept warm by her body. It is a strange world to be on the outside, it is colder and most of the time noisier as well. Most of the time, this will resolve on its own as the baby grows and gets accustomed to life on the outside. One possible solution parents could try is to work with different swaddles or rockers.

Sleep Accessories

Monitors

With the development of new technology, came the era of monitors. No longer do parents have to guess whether their baby is sleeping or not, there are various monitors that allow caretakers to see or hear the baby from another room. Plenty more have been developed which provide further information such as whether the baby is breathing.

The choice on which ones to purchase lies solely with the parents and what options fit the family best. There are some important points to remember when choosing a monitor, besides the type, such as:

- Audio monitors – these are relatively inexpensive monitors that provide only audio feedback. In most instances, the audio goes both ways, allowing parents to sooth the baby before they reach it. Most of these are also equipped with a light-up option, which means that as the baby makes noise that the monitor picks up, it will also light up based on the intensity of the noise.

- Audio and Video monitors – monitors such as these are also equipped with a small camera that can be mounted on a wall or set up on a surface. They are either in black and white or color and provide not just the sound of the baby, but a visual as well. They are a tad more expensive than the regular audio monitors but provide parents with the extra security of seeing their baby sleep soundly. It allows the parents or a caretaker to ensure that the baby hasn't moved, twisted, or otherwise found themselves in a predicament that may be dangerous.

- Wireless network monitors – these are digital monitors that work off an existing wireless connection. The receiver, instead of a small screen, is a device that works off the wireless network such as a computer, tablet, or phone. Since the receiver can be a tablet or a phone, it allows the parents to see their baby from further away, so long as there is an internet connection.

- Movement monitors – are designed specifically to alert parents if their baby has not moved for more than twenty seconds or so and are a little more on the costly side. In order to be effective, this type of monitor comes equipped with a motion sensor pad that is slipped underneath the mattress. It is designed to be sensitive enough to feel the baby's breathing and other movements. Besides monitors that come with pads underneath the mattress, there are others that are in the form of a sock that the baby wears overnight. There have been no studies performed on whether they are any more effective in the prevention of SIDS and have been formally recommended by neither AAP nor NIH (National Institute of Health).

Though the monitors that are available to parents nowadays are as fancy as they can get, by alerting to troublesome breathing or simply when the baby has woken, there are many people out there that are opting out of the use of baby monitors. Of course, to any new parent, the technology sounds amazing and unbelievably helpful, however, many soon find out that it is not all it is cracked up to be.

Babies will make noise no matter what, especially when they are sleeping, meaning that the monitor will pick up every breath, hiccup, or gurgle that a baby makes, waking parents more often than it should. Movement monitors tend to malfunction, or those with socks slip off as the baby moves in its sleep, again, rousing parents unintentionally, as well as scaring them in the process. It is due to those simple facts that parents are beginning to ditch their monitors. They found themselves rushing in too many times, even if the baby wasn't awake and reacting prematurely.

Swaddles

Swaddling a baby means to wrap the baby tightly in a blanket or special swaddle which are currently out on the market. There are a couple of good reasons why swaddling is prominent.

- Stops the baby from being scared by their own startle reflex which can last even up to 6 months.

- Studies have been performed which have found that the act of swaddling a baby could actually help prevent SIDS.

- Keeps the baby warm when the baby cannot use a blanket since anything soft in the crib is not advisable.

- May help to calm the baby. Some parents have found that their baby is much easier to put to sleep when they've been swaddled.

If the baby came into the world at a hospital, you will see the nurses come and swaddle the baby. Before leaving the hospital, it is best to get pointers from those nurses on how to best swaddle a baby and they would be very happy to oblige. It is best to ensure that you are swaddling correctly before you bring your baby home and put them to bed. When using a blanket as a swaddle, ensure that you are following the correct swaddling steps.

- Use a square blanket that has been made for swaddling. Lay the blanket down on a flat surface and fold down the top corner.

- Lay the baby down on their back and ensure that the top part of the blanket is at shoulder height.

- Place the baby's left arm down, then pull the corner of the blanket nearest the left hand over the arms and the chest of the baby, then tuck the edge under their back on the right side.

- Next, bring down the baby's right arm and pull the corner nearest the right hand over the arm and chest and tuck it in on the left side.

- Twist the bottom of the blanket and tuck it behind the baby, leaving enough room for the baby to bend both their legs out naturally. This is done to ensure that the baby does not develop hip dysplasia.

Though swaddling is a practice that has been taking place for millennia, it is still best to be advised on all the aspects of the practice before making the decision to continue the process beyond the hospital stay.

- Opposite to what most parents think, a baby does not have to be swaddled. If you find that your baby has no trouble falling asleep and staying asleep without a swaddle, do not bother continuing on with the process. This will only lead to the issue of having to break the habit later.

- Make certain that you put the baby to sleep on their back. In turn, swaddling should stop the moment that the baby shows any signs of turning over on to their tummy. If a baby were to find itself in that position, they would have trouble lifting their head enough to be able to breathe comfortably.

- Though the baby's legs need to have some freedom of movement to ensure correct development, you have to make sure that the swaddle is nice and snug and cannot come loose. A loose swaddle could pose a suffocation hazard.

Due to these different criteria, different swaddles have been developed to help make the process easier. There are many different swaddles out there, therefore, some research and trial and error may be necessary as not all babies will take to the same swaddle. The best thing to keep in mind is to use a swaddle that will allow the baby to move around their legs and hips.

No matter the type of swaddle used, or even if it's just a blanket, it is best to take into consideration all of the options that are out there. Also, as the caregivers, you have to remember that a swaddle cannot be used forever, even if it makes bedtime much easier. A baby will start to roll sooner or later, and it is at that time they will need to have more freedom while sleeping to ensure that they do not run into the risk of suffocation.

Other Accessories

Besides accessories such as monitors or swaddles, other items have been developed that are said to help the baby sleep. There is no written rule that states that these must be purchased, and in some instances, parents may even want to think twice about doing so.

The first item to be mentioned is a soother whether it uses noise or vibrations. Some of these come as combination soothers, which means that the item does both white background noise and vibration. There are also plenty out there that do either one or the other. Most parents will gravitate towards a white noise machine, believing that it will help drown out the noise of the rest of the house, allowing the baby to doze off and stay asleep.

There is even an entire bassinet developed which gently rocks the baby, makes a white noise of some sort and vibrates helping the baby fall asleep. Another bassinet was developed to mimic a ride in the car where it is said babies fall asleep the best.

Though these items may work wonders, they are also something a baby can get very used to and have trouble falling asleep without. This may become problematic as the baby grows and it is clear that they should no longer have to use sleep aids, or they've simply outgrown the item. For example, the bassinet mentioned above will one day be something that a baby outgrows. Since it had been doing most of the work for the parents when it comes to putting the baby to sleep for the night, it will not be an easy process breaking that habit. It may be best to teach the baby how to self soothe from early on, even if it means that there may be some hours of lost sleep.

One more item that is worth mentioning here is a humidifier or an essential oil diffuser; some have even been combined. A humidifier that is used to bring more moisture into the area can be very helpful around dry seasons. They assist the baby to breathe a little easier during those times, making sleep a more comfortable process. If the humidifier has an option to be used as an essential oil diffuser, it becomes an added bonus

Sleep outside the home

Neither parents nor the baby can be expected to remain indoors until the child is older. Life continues on, and especially when there are older siblings involved, parents will find that the baby needs to start leaving the house with them right away.

Since, as mentioned earlier, babies sleep most of the time their first few weeks of life, when a baby leaves the house, they will need somewhere to continue on their slumber which is so very important in the beginning.

The length of the trip will determine the best options for a baby, with shorter trips obviously needing less.

- Infant car seat: when leaving the home, to go on a short trip such as a store or to visit a friend or relative, parents will need to take the baby in a car seat. A majority of parents will use an infant cart seat. This type of car seat has a base that has been pre-installed into the car and that can be clipped into the base or into a stroller. This makes it easier to move baby from one place to another, especially if there are a couple of tips in between, such as running errands. A baby can safely slumber in their seat while they are being moved between the car and either store or home. It is, however, important to remember that w long car trips, a baby needs to be removed from their seat every so often. Also, an infant car seat should only be used when clipped into either a car or the stroller so that it sits at the optimal angle. Babies are at risk for asphyxiation if they are left in their car seat which is set down for example, on the floor, without the base or the stroller.

- Stroller: some strollers come with either an attached or built-in bassinet. This means that the stroller fully reclines in a laydown position allowing a newborn to sleep laying down much like they would in an actual bassinet or crib. It is convenient if you are staying in one spot for a long period of time, such as if you are going for a walk or a shopping mall. This does not allow for an easy transfer from car to store or home, but it does provide the baby with a safe and flat way of sleeping. Something like this can also be used if you are visiting someone and setting up the stroller instead of a pack-and-play as an example.

- Travel beds: besides the pack-and-play that has been mentioned already, there are smaller portable travel beds out there. Some are even disguised as a diaper bag with just as many pockets to work as both. These are strictly for the newborn as they are relatively small in comparison to even a real bassinet. They do allow the convenience of being able to put the baby down anywhere, whether it's just outside the home, at someone's house, the airport, plane, or hotel. The possibilities with such a bed, so long as space is provided, are endless.

Newborn babies sleep almost anywhere, they just have to be provided with a safe space to do so. For short trips, an infant car seat is perfect especially when running errands and the baby will need to be moved between the car and a store repeatedly within a short length of time. Car seats, however, cannot be used as nap space if they are brought inside and placed anywhere but the stroller or base they are designed for.

There are, of course, other options such as the stroller itself or a travel bed designed specifically to allow the baby to lay in a flat position as is dictated by safe sleep practices.

Takeaway

Unfortunately, there is no one right answer for the way a baby does or does not sleep, whether they should be monitored while they do, whether they should be swaddled or not, or what actions to take if parents feel there is a problem.

Things to remember are that sleep safe is the most important aspect of putting the baby down to sleep, whether they sleep through the night or not. Most newborns will not be sleeping through the night for a couple of months, and that does not mean there is anything wrong. Their small stomachs mean that they will get hungry faster and it is best to provide them with whatever they need at the moment.

In most instances, it becomes a trial error on the part of the parents. It is, however, not recommended to sleep train a newborn. Sleep training, and there are many schools of thought on this, is something that can take place at a later time when the baby has gotten older and understands more of its world. For now, at the newborn stage, if the baby requires just extra food or more cuddles, parents should focus on providing that the best that they can. One day the baby will be older, a toddler, teenager, or grown-up, and will no longer need that extra care to get to sleep.

CHAPTER 4:

Cleaning Baby

Another tip to parents in the long journey of caring for their newborn is cleaning the baby, which can be either a fun experience or one that parents find daunting. A baby's first bath becomes a major milestone for parents, but it comes with many uncertainties. With so many bathing options out there, as well as advice on best practices, it can quickly become very overwhelming. The hope here is to put some of that to rest.

First and foremost, it is best to keep in mind that a bath should become a pleasant experience, even if in the beginning the baby may appear not to like it all that much. It is a chance for the baby to bond with its parents as this is a task that can be performed by either parent. In some situations, if a mother is breastfeeding, this is something that can be left for the dad to do so that he too can be as involved as possible.

Babies tend to feel safer in the arms of their dad which is what helps the two of them bond. Dad can make bath time as additional time that he gets to spend with the baby, especially if the dad is the one that is working outside of the home mostly.

Top and Tail

Topping and tailing refer to washing the baby's head, neck, hands, and bottom. Most of the time it is a process that is employed when the baby's umbilical cord has not fallen off and parents do not want to submerge the baby in water to give it a bath.

Some parents also choose to continue this process in between baths as baby's do not require baths as many times throughout the week as an adult. Since baby's do not move around as much, and therefore, do not sweat as much, unless necessary for others reason (such as a really bad diaper) on average babies get baths around two to three times in a week. There are some simple steps for this process:

1. Before starting to undress the baby, make sure that you have everything in hand such as a clean diaper, clothes, a towel, a soft cotton rag for washing, and that the room is sufficiently warm.

2. Only a small bowl of water is needed for this process. The water should not be too hot or too cold. If need

be, check the water temperature with your elbow as it is a good indicator of how the baby will feel the temperature of the water.

3. After the baby is undressed, it is best to leave the baby on top of a soft towel so that she can be dried right away and kept from getting too cold.

4. Dampening the soft cotton rag, begin with the face using soft and gentle touches, working your way down, and covering the baby as you go.

5. Some parents decide to use gentle baby soap on the genitals and bottom to ensure thorough cleanliness from any poop that the baby may have done.

6. Once you consider the baby to be cleaned, she can be placed back into a diaper and the chosen outfit to keep warm.

The directions above can be used as a general guideline and may be adjusted based on the needs of the situation or the baby. Parents will find that this process will become intuitive with practice.

First Bath

Technically, a baby's first bath would be given at the hospital by the nurse, who can also show how the process is done having had many years of practice. Each hospital has different practices when it comes to a first bath, so it is best to ask ahead of time in case you would like to do something different.

In some hospitals, a baby's first bath is given as soon as possible since the baby is coated in different fluids upon entry into the world. However, there are parents that have been choosing to delay that bath at the hospital for up to 48 hours. This decision is made based on the recommendation of doctors who have provided the following information.

- Reduces the risk of infection: this is because delaying the bath leaves the baby covered in what is called vernix in which they are born. Vernix is a white substance that is made up of skin cells which the baby made while they were developing in utero and this coating actually works as an antibiotic ointment, warding off bacteria.

- Assists in stabilizing blood sugar: when the baby is cut off from the placenta, it loses that which had stabilized their blood sugar all of that time. When placed in a bath, babies tend to get stressed which causes the release of hormones which cause blood sugar to drop, a dangerous thing in an infant.

- Helps with temperature control: in some instances, bathing the baby soon causes the baby to go into hypothermia because they are unable to control their own body temperature when they are born. This is also why babies are kept bundled up or under heat lamps in the hospital.

- Improved bonding and breastfeeding: studies have shown that babies tend to do better with bonding and breastfeeding when they are allowed to stay with their mother without the intervention of medical procedures. In a hospital, a bath would also be called a medical procedure, and it is one that can wait for those precious first hours.

- Moisturizer: vernix works like a natural moisturizer for the skin. Bathing the baby will only remove that moisturizer and it cannot be substituted with anything else.

- Parent special time: by allowing the mother to recover from her ordeal, she is able to participate in that special time between the baby and caregiver. If she would like this to take place at the hospital, the nurse is also there to assist and provide guidance.

The bath that is given to a baby in the hospital as a first bath, will not necessarily appear the same as it does at home. This type of bath is usually what has been described above as a top and tail. Since the baby's umbilical stump still remains attached, the baby cannot be submerged. This also allows the parents to have that special first bath at home if this is not something that they were able to participate in at the hospital.

The first bath at home has become almost a rite of passage, a big milestone for a baby, the moment that parents feel their baby is ready. There are no right answers as to when the baby may be ready, but most parents look for at least the umbilical cord to fall off to ensure that it does not get submerged in water.

The Where

The biggest decision with giving the baby a bath is whereas the options would include a baby bath (if one was purchased), a regular bath, or the sink. Either will be perfectly adequate, it will all just depend on what works best for the family. For parents who have a small space, purchasing a baby bathtub may not be a feasible option, and there is nothing wrong with that.

In those instances, it is best to stick to the bathtub or sink. In some cases, a parent can also give the baby a shower, by showering right along with them. A bath can be given to the baby by itself in the big tub, using small amounts of water, or by taking a bath with the baby. A bath can be a scary experience for a baby in the beginning and taking a bath with a parent could be a soothing experience.

However, for the parents that decided they would feel more comfortable with a baby bathtub, there are different options to consider:

- Bathtubs that work as sink inserts. They are usually flexible and fit into most standard-sized sinks. Since they go into a sink, they are perfectly at the height for a standing adult and does not require leaning over.

- Standard tubs are standalone bathtubs made to fit children of various sizes and can be placed on the ground or a table or counter.

- Convertible tubs which are standalone tubs that have the ability to convert from newborn to toddler use.

- Hammock bathtubs are just that, regular standalone bathtubs that come with a mesh hammock for babies that are unable to support themselves.

- The inflatable tub is a space saver as it is blown up with air like an outdoor small pool.

- A fold-up tub is also a space saver like the inflatable tub. It is usually a hard tub, but it folds for easy storage. Most of these tubs can also be used from the newborn stage through toddlerhood.

- A bucket tub is a plastic bin that resembles more of a bucket than it does a bathtub, but it is designed to hold the baby in an upright position, much like a sink could.

There is no right answer when it comes to choosing the right tub and it is something that can be held off until the baby has arrived since a baby does not get a bath the moment that they are home. One can go as fancy or as simple as they feel like, or not purchase one at all.

When moving forward with actually making the purchase, if, at all possible, it's best to research the different types of tubs and how they work, even asking others for testimonials on their tubs. This may help in narrowing down which of the tubs mentioned above would meet the needs of the family and the baby specifically.

The How

Once the desired area is chosen, the essentials for a bath are much the same as they are for a top and tail. The items that are most needed are a change of diaper, clothes, towel, soft rag to wash the baby with, and gentle baby soap. Again, it is best to ensure that the area the baby is bathed in is a warm one to prevent any colds.

Whether the baby is using its own bathtub, a regular bathtub, or the sink, there needs to be no more than around two inches of water. This will be enough water to ensure that the baby is kept warm throughout the experience, but not enough that they may become fully submerged on their own. Some simple tips can be provided for a good bathing experience:

- Gather all of your things in the area chosen for changing baby whether that is a changing table or bed. This way, once the baby is washed there will be no reason to waste time, preventing the baby from becoming cold.

- Ensure that the baby is kept warm throughout the experience by placing a small towel on top of the baby during the bath. Periodically, warm the towel in the bathwater and only take it off as you wash each area.

- It is best to use baby soap sparingly. This is to prevent the baby's skin from drying out or risking any type of skin outbreak should they be allergic.

- Always keep at least one hand on the baby in case the baby starts to slip. Never leave the baby unattended in the bath. If you find yourself needing to walk away, take the baby with you.

- After the baby is bathed, moisturize the baby's skin using either a special baby lotion or coconut oil.

Though a bath can seem daunting sometimes, there are only a few quick steps that need to be followed. All in all, as parents you just have to ensure that the baby is being bathed in a safe environment that is not too hot. A bath can be given as sparingly or as many times in a week as you would deem necessary.

The Benefits

Generally speaking, baby's like to take baths as long as it is a relaxing process, that is why some parents tend to incorporate that into the night time routine as the baby starts getting older.

There are certain benefits to bathing the baby, whether it is something that parents decide to do daily or only two or three times a week. These benefits are more than just a clean baby at the end of the day.

- It helps with the parent-baby bond. Bath time can become a special time in the day between the baby and the parent. Both of you have to be focused on each other, the baby on the parent that is bathing it and the parent on the baby. There is time to have skin to skin contact, especially if you choose to have a bath or shower with your baby. When being bathed by mom, babies also like to feed if they are breastfed, facilitating that bond together.

- Bathing can become a learning experience for the baby. There are plenty of different toys available for bath time that can help with baby's development such as learning shapes or colors. Babies also learn to use their imaginations in the tub and learn to play with the water for later use in a pool scenario.

- Relaxes a baby that has become agitated. Throughout the day, a baby can become overstimulated learning different things and growing. A nice calm bath with a parent helps the baby calm down before they are put to bed for the night. It's also a good way to introduce a baby massage to be given after the bath with the use of moisturizers.

- It helps the baby get ready for bed. There is a reason that parents start to introduce a bath, whether recommended daily or not, into a bedtime routine. The warmth of the water and the calmness of the situation helps babies get ready for sleep.

The Challenges

Like anything in life, even something as simple as bathing a baby can come with its own set of challenges. It's important to remember that a bath does not need to take place daily if this is something that has become a source of contention. Since each baby grows at their own rate, sometimes it is best to allow the baby to let you know when they are ready for something, such as taking baths more often.

Though most babies take to a bath right away, there are some babies that are not fond of bath time. If the baby gets very agitated at bath time, it is a good idea to check some things off the list to determine the cause.

- Check the temperature of the water. The baby may not be happy as the water is either too hot or too cold.

- The next time you bathe the baby, feed the baby first to ensure it just isn't hunger that is causing them distress.

- Try giving the baby a bath after a nap, or not too long after to rule out whether the baby has just been overtired and in no mood for bathing.

- The baby may just not feel safe in the water on their own or want the company. Taking a bath or shower with the baby is also an option to try and rule out baby discomfort.

Unfortunately, there are those babies that no matter the effort on the part of the parents, are just not fond of baths and may not be for a while yet. If that is the case, the best thing to do is to give fewer baths, since newborns don't require many to begin with and to try and give them as quickly as possible. Undress the baby right beside the tub or sink to minimize the bathing process and possible amount of time they feel cold.

Though the baby may cry, there is no reason to become discouraged. As time progresses, and the baby grows, baths will become an event that the family will look forward to, filled with bubbles, toys, and fun.

Product Guidelines

When the baby is born it is protected by the vernix, a white substance that the baby forms in utero which protects the skin from outside elements. It works like a very well-made moisturizer. Well, after the baby's first birth, whether it's a cleaning given by the hospital or one at home, that vernix disappears. From there, the care of the baby's skin falls on the parents and the products they use.

One product is not equal to another as studies have shown us in the past. Recently, there has been a rise in products that are mostly natural due to people's fear of chemicals. The same type of care should be given to the choice made by parents regarding the products they use on their babies.

As a result of studies performed on various chemicals and baby products, it has been determined that there are quite a few chemicals that people have been using on their babies without giving them a second thought. Products that we used to believe are safe, may no longer be considered so.

- Talc: this is a powdered mineral that is commonly used in baby powder, a product that had been considered a staple in every home with a baby. Though talc works great as a drying substance, hence it's used on baby bottoms, it has been proven to be a lung irritant.

- Fragrance: many products on the shelves, whether for babies or adults, have an added fragrance which is supposed to kill off the smell of the chemicals that are used to make the products itself. The problem with the use of the term is that it encompasses any chemicals that the company uses, without disclosing the information in depth. However, most of these fragrances are based on coal or petroleum. Due to their design, they linger on the skin and are a common cause of respiratory, neurological, skin, or eye damage. In some cases, there has been evidence that the use of such fragrances can lead children to develop asthma. The biggest problem here is that they linger, and babies tend to put things in their mouths, their own skin being number one on the list.

- Propylene Glycol: this chemical allows the product to be easily absorbed by the skin which pretty much means that this product will open the pores of the baby and allow things to sink in further. As an added perspective, propylene glycol is also a substance used in the windshield wiper fluid.

- 1,4 -dioxane and ethylated surfactants: studies performed by the Environmental Working Group showed that as many as 57% of baby products are made with this substance. This substance is actually a by-product when ethylene oxide is used to make other chemicals less harsh, but it in and of itself is a carcinogen.

- Mineral oil: this substance is a by-product that happens when petroleum is processed making it act like a plastic wrap around the skin. This type of chemical is usually found in baby oil and should be avoided at all costs. A better alternative is something along the lines of olive or coconut oil.

- Parabens: these chemicals are linked to various issues such as reproductive toxicity, hormone disruption, and skin irritation. Unfortunately, this is a substance that is found almost everywhere, even if the product is marketed at babies.

- Triclosan: this pertains more or less to any product that is labeled as being antibacterial. This substance is considered a carcinogen and is harmful to the environment.

Due to the fact that studies have been performed and determined the above list of chemicals as the top ones to avoid, there are plenty of options out there that can be considered chemical-free. In some instances, it is even best to forgo buying a "beauty" product altogether as there are safer alternatives. As mentioned above, instead of using something like baby oil, coconut oil is a great alternative. This is something that can be purchased right off the shelf of a grocery store and will most likely not cost much more than a baby moisturizer.

Now that a thorough review of what should be avoided has been done, there are a couple of things to look for when purchasing baby bath products.

- Fewer ingredients: the smaller the list of ingredients on the back of the product, the better the product will be. Partially, this is because you will be able to make a much more informed decision. Unless someone is particularly knowledgeable about all of the ingredients, it is best to go with the shorter list of chemicals you understand more.

- Eco-friendly: make the choice be a product that is friendly to the environment as a whole and not just the one person. This is because anything that you used to wash with, whether it be yourself or your baby, gets washed down the drain and goes back into the environment.

- Unscented products: as mentioned above, fragrances carry chemicals that are harmful not just to the person, but the environment as well. It is best to go for the products that advertise themselves as being fragrance-free.

- "All-purpose" products: this could be products that are advertised as a body wash and shampoo in one, which most of the baby products are. This helps keep down your own cost of product and saves the environment in various ways.

An alternative to trying to buy products that you feel comfortable with is making your own. Do-it-yourself products are at an all-time high since people trust it more. If you make the product yourself, you will obviously be aware of what you have used to make it. It can also become cost-efficient in the long run as most of the products you will buy to combine together you will purchase in bulk.

It only makes sense that with the studies that have been performed in the very recent past, people would shy away from as many chemicals as possible. This is especially true of parents who want to ensure that their babies are taken care of as best as possible.

Bath accessories

Babies come with all sorts of adorable accessories for every portion of their day and bathing is no different. There are many small and big accessories out there that can be purchased for bath time that may make it more enjoyable for both the parent and the baby.

- A hooded towel: though, of course, a towel is necessary to dry off and keep the baby warm, hooded towels are a bit of a novelty. They come in all sorts of patterns, whether they turn your baby in a lion or an elephant and are usually purchased just for sheer decoration.

- Bath toys: though a baby will not be able to pick up any toys yet, they can provide a good distraction and source of bonding time. Most of the first baby bath toys to be purchased are squeezable toys that squirt water. It is best to buy those that have a removable top to ensure that they can be properly cleaned and that mold will not form on the inside.

- Cups: these are specifically cups that help rinse the baby, especially the baby's head which not all babies are a fan of. It can be a regular looking cup with a cute pattern or more of a novelty such as in the shape of a whale that spits water. This is something that can be used on the baby as they grow making washing the head a better experience for all.

- A thermometer: though an elbow will do just as well at checking the temperature of the water before you place the baby in it, there are thermometers designed specifically to show you the temperature of the water in many different shapes. For example, some come in the shape of ducks or turtles that will even advise if the temperature is getting too hot.

- Knee pads: this is more specific for parents, but there are knee pads, and in some instances, a combination of knee pads and elbow pads, to help you kneel beside the tub in comfort and give the baby a bath.

- No-slip mat: this is a rubber mat that suctions to the bottom of the tub to help the baby from slipping around. This is also something that could be used by the whole family.

In the very beginning, bath toys and accessories are just a novelty, they are not necessarily things that are needed in order to actually bathe the baby. Some things such as baby toys or the no-split mat are something that can continue being used down the road as the baby grows into a toddler making the investment something worthwhile.

Takeaway

Bath time can become a good source of a bonding experience between the baby and its parents or caregivers. There is one uniform way in which to give a baby a bath as it can be given in an actual tub, a baby bathtub, or the sink. There are also many different baby bathtubs out there to choose from should parents take that route.

What is important to remember is that though a bath can be a bonding experience, it does not have to happen often. It is best for the baby's skin if they are not bathed daily so as not to strip the baby's skin of its natural moisture. This means that when the baby is bathed it is important to moisture afterward. As mentioned, this can also be a good time to provide the baby with a small massage.

All in all, bathing a baby can become a great and wholesome experience, but some babies still don't like to bathe. That does not mean that the parents have done anything wrong, as there are no right or wrong answers here, but the baby may just need more time to grow into the idea. Slowly and steadily, it can be introduced and any fears on the part of the parent of the baby can be overcome.

CHAPTER 5:

Caring for Newborn Belly Button

The Umbilical Cord

An umbilical cord is what connects the baby to its mother inside of the womb. The cord runs from a hole in the baby's stomach and is connected to the placenta allowing it to carry vital nutrients from mother to the baby. On average, an umbilical cord is twenty inches long and is made up of one vein and two arteries.

The vein in the umbilical cord is what carries the oxygenated blood and nutrients from mom to the baby. On the other hand, the arteries return the deoxygenated blood and any waste products from the baby back to the placenta. At the end of the pregnancy, the cord will also supply the baby with antibodies made by the mother which will help protect the baby for up to three months after their birth.

After a baby is born, the cord will be clamped off about three or four inches away from the belly of the baby with a plastic clip. Next, the cord is clamped off close to the placenta and cut somewhere between the two clamps. The umbilical cord will then turn in to a stump that is roughly two to three inches in length. With a vaginal birth, the mother's partner is able to cut the cord should they request to do so, otherwise, it will be either the nurse, doctor, or midwife.

Possible Medical Cord Issues

Though the risk of umbilical cord issues, before or during the birth, taking place are very minor, in some instances as small as one percent, they should still be mentioned. These are conditions that can only be diagnosed by a doctor, in some instances with the use of ultrasound technology while the mother is still pregnant. In the end, however, none of these would impact the care that is given to the umbilical cord stump once the baby is at home and resting.

- Umbilical cord prolapse: this happens when the cord slips into the birth canal ahead of the baby and may become pinched. If your water were to break at home, it is best to head into the hospital, not just to ward off any possible bacteria, but to ensure that you are being monitored by doctors as the water first has to break before this is ever possible.

- Single umbilical artery: this is diagnosed when one of the arteries of the umbilical cord is missing. Unfortunately, there is no known reason why this happens, therefore, it is not something that can be prevented.

- Vasa Previa: this condition happens when one or more blood vessels from either the umbilical cord or the placenta cross the cervix.

- Nuchal cord: is when the cord wraps itself around the baby's neck which can be seen on an ultrasound. Most of the time, babies with a nuchal cord are born quite healthy.

- Umbilical cord knots: usually these knots form into the umbilical cord in the beginning of the pregnancy when the baby is able to move around more freely. Knots can be diagnosed by your doctor during routine ultrasounds of the baby during pregnancy. In most cases, if one is diagnosed, to ensure that the baby and the mother stay safe, a c-section will be performed.

- Umbilical cord cysts: these are sacks that are full of fluid within the umbilical cord. They are not that common as only less than one percent off pregnancies are diagnosed with this. Any cyst that is diagnosed already in the third trimester does not pose a danger to the baby.

Caring for a newborn belly button

The stump of the belly button will fall off on its own within five to fifteen days from the birth of the baby. Once the stump has fallen off, the belly button will fully heal within seven to ten days. At first, the cord may appear to be yellow in color and as it dries it will turn to a greyish, or even purple, color. Those are all quite normal, as it will eventually shrivel and turn in to a black color before it falls off.

Though doctors used to recommend that the base of the stump is cleaned with rubbing alcohol, that has since changed. Nowadays, doctors advise parents to leave the stump alone, allowing it to dry and fall off on its own. If you find that the stump, or the area nearby appears too wet, you may dry it very gently with something like a Q-Tip and check that the baby is normally clothed in something breathable like cotton.

The one thing that parents have to remember is to keep the area dry, which means no fully submerged baths until the cord is gone and the area has healed. To ensure that it is healed properly, it is best not to pick at the stump even if appears to be hanging on by a thread. As soon as it is ready, it will fall off on its own, giving way for the belly button to hear naturally.

In the context of keeping the area dry, it is best to allow the stump to have air time as often as is possible. This means that any diaper that a baby is wearing is either cut specifically to allow the stump freedom or folding the diaper right below it. If it is feasible, it is also good to allow the baby to have some naked time. During the naked time, it is best to ensure that the baby will not go cold, therefore, any room that they are kept in should be kept warm and away from any drafts. This does not have to be a long length of time as it can be for just a couple of minutes during the day.

Possible Belly Button Problems

Besides leaving the cord to its own ministrations, the parent should be on the lookout for a possible infection. There are a couple of signs that would help distinguish if the stump or belly button is infected and require medical attention:

- The base of the stump appears to be overly red or becomes swollen

- The cord continued to bleed

- There is yellow ooze or discharge from the belly button

- It holds a foul smell

- The baby seems to be reacting in pain if it is grazed or touched

Since any infection of the umbilical cord can give rise to what is called omphalitis. Omphalitis an infection of the umbilical cord and it is considered a life-threatening condition. As such, it should be treated immediately. It is best to call the pediatricians office to get the next steps on a possible appointment or immediate care instructions.

Another condition that affects the umbilical cord is what is called an umbilical granuloma. It is a small nodule that is usually pink or red in color which has a persistent yellow-green discharge. With a granuloma, there will be no swelling, redness, or fever to indicate that there is in fact anything wrong. If it is suspected that the baby has a granuloma, it is best to bring the baby to their pediatrician. In most cases, it is treated with silver nitrate which cauterizes the area. Since there are no nerve endings there, there is no need to worry as the baby will not feel any pain.

Lastly, the one question that parents find themselves asking quite often is whether there is a way to ensure that their baby has what is considered an "innie" instead of an "outie" belly button. Though in the past people have placed a coin over the belly button to help it go in, it is in fact proven that this will not help. Since the best thing for the belly button is to be left alone to heal, placing something like a coin is definitely not advisable, nor does it actually work.

There are times when a belly button that protrudes outward, or the "outie", can be a sign of a problem. Sometimes, the formation of the belly button in such a way is a sign of what is called an umbilical hernia. An umbilical hernia happens when the intestines and the surrounding fat are protruding through the muscles of the stomach and push out under the belly button. Though it takes a medical professional to diagnose a hernia, it is generally painless and will resolve on its own within at most a few years.

What to do with the stump?

As the stump of the umbilical cord starts to dry and wither away, everyone takes a different approach to the process and what that means later. Some parents will be overjoyed at finally being able to give their newborn a proper bath, one they hope is filled with love and giggles. There are those parents, however, that hope to save it, as they may other things.

For those parents that decide to put the stump somewhere other than the immediate garbage can, there are options for its safekeeping that are both practical and adorable.

- Scrapbook or memory book: this is the easiest approach as there are many options out there that have space for the umbilical stump to be placed.

Before taping it in, however, be sure that it is thoroughly dried or place it in a baggie if you are not sure.

- Bury it: some cultures have adapted the burying of the stump from generation to generation. There are also moms that have started the practice even if it is not their cultural norm by burying the stump somewhere and placing a plant on top whether a tree, bush, or flowers.

- Jewelry: much as breastmilk can be turned in to jewelry, so can the umbilical stump. There are companies out there that will transform the stump into a beautiful looking piece of jewelry that can be worn by the mother. Jewelers that specialize in this type of work can make various pieces out of the stump such as a necklace or ring.

- Frame it: this option could include more than just the umbilical stump. A shadowbox is a great idea for placing baby items into and hanging it on a wall for either personal or public display.

- Toy (or something of the like): this means sewing the stump into a favorite toy or lovey, most likely once the child outgrows the toy. This allows the parents to keep the toy and give it to their child once they are grown.

All of these options are safe and are something that can be passed down to the child once the time is right as they won't understand the significance until they are much older.

The option to save the stump is not for everyone, of course, and no one should feel that they need to do so. Though it may be an amazing thing to look back on in later years, it may be more amazing for the mother rather than anyone else like the grown child.

Takeaway

When mom and baby are still one, with the baby safely tucked away inside the womb, the umbilical cord is what gives the baby life. Though there are some medical issues that can happen with this life-giving cord, they are very few and far between and do not need any further thought unless brought up by the doctor.

The important thing to remember about the stump and the belly button is that for the most part, it takes care of itself, as long as it receives some gentle treatment. It has been designed to fall off on its own within a couple of days from the birth of the baby as long as it is kept dry and not overly restricted. If anything at all looks amiss, it is best to contact the pediatrician right away for further information on treatment.

CHAPTER 6:

Clothing baby

Clothing a baby, whether they are for a boy or a girl, is one of the tasks that parents look forward to the most. The outfits that are available for any gender are absolutely adorable, however, there are so many choices and so many things to keep in mind when making purchases.

When it comes to newborns, preparation really does matter, hence the institution of having a baby shower. Not only is a time for others to come and join the parents on such a joyous occasion and show their support, but it is also a wonderful way for parents to prepare as much as possible for their bundle of joy that will join them in the world soon.

Clothing is one of the most purchased items for a baby shower whether the parents have found out the gender ahead of time, or they are remaining gender-neutral until the baby is born. What this means for the parents is that because it is difficult to predict the sizes that will be needed once the baby is born, it is best to buy the minimum at first as others will have already added on to the pile of newborn clothes whether we asked them to or not.

Types of outfits available and how many needed

Before either shopping for the clothes ourselves or placing them on to a baby shower registration, be cognizant of the sizes that are out there. First and foremost, each brand has specifics when it comes to the sizes of their clothes, therefore, it is best to look closely. Most brands will actually list not just the size on the tag, but how big baby has to be in order to fit into those sizes best. There is usually a weight and length measurement provided on the tag underneath the size pointing you in the right direction.

In the first few weeks of life, newborns will grow exponentially. At first, the baby is growing in order to make up the weight that they lost after birth, and then later they will continue to grow, moving up from one size to another pretty quickly. By around five months or so, the baby should have doubled in weight, definitely outgrowing most of their first baby clothes by that time.

Remember, some babies are born on the smaller side which means that they will fit into preemie clothes, and some are born a little later which means that they will outgrow the newborn size relatively fast. Therefore, the number of clothes that you will need to settle on depends on the number of times in a week that you will want to focus on doing laundry. Based on the recommendations below, if you plan on doing laundry only once in a week, it is best to double the amount recommended. If you wash clothes every day, as is in some families, you can take the amount recommended and cut it by half.

- Bodysuits or Rompers: these types of outfits are usually the staple in any baby closet. During the summer months, they can be used as a quick light outfit, and in the winter, they can be used as a base to keep the baby warm since they do come in a long-sleeve option. The recommended amount to have on hand is about seven.

- Pants: at the newborn age, most babies do not wear pants unless it is chilly outside, therefore it is good to have at least three pairs on hand.

- Hats: there are plenty of hats that come with outfits and do not have to be purchased separately, however, since newborns are still learning to regulate their body temperature, it is best to have two on hand for the first weeks.

- Socks: since babies cannot walk, they don't really need socks unless it is winter and exceptionally cold.

It is best to have around five pairs of socks and it is best to get them all in one color. With as small as baby socks are, they tend to get lost pretty quickly as well.

- Swaddles: though these are not necessarily considered clothing that baby will wear out, it is best to have two or three on hand if you are choosing to swaddle the baby in the middle of the night. Do your research on different types of swaddles out there, however, since they can be very specific to be baby size, meaning that if the baby is born on the smaller end, they will most likely need to wait to use it.

- Sleepers (pajamas): these come in footed, non-footed, or gowns options and it is best to have around four on hand of any of these. These are great for playtime or can be used inside a swaddle as well. They are cozy and great insulators for the baby during colder days or nights.

- Sweaters: this includes any sweatshirt type shirts. It is best to have two sweaters on hand whether they are cardigan or zippered. Since the baby cannot be placed into a car seat with a jacket or bunting, this can be used as an added layer to ward off the cold.

- Mittens: depending on how much the baby leaves the house during the colder months, it is best to have two pairs of warmer mittens on hand. For year-round use, there are mittens out there specifically designed so that the baby doesn't cut themselves with their fingernails until they can be cut. It is best to have two of those on hand as well.

Specifically, for the winter months, it is best to have the following on hand as well:

- Winter coat: this can be either an actual jacket or a bunting which may be easier to use for a newborn. Only one of these is needed, but be aware that in most of these outfits the baby should not be placed into a car seat. Due to the bulkiness of such clothing, the car seat straps will not sit close enough to the chest and could cause the baby to fly out of the seat in case of an accident. They do come in handy when taking the baby for a walk in a stroller, however.

- Slippers (booties): these will not be used for walking, but a pair can come in handy if it is cold and baby's feet need to be kept warm outside, such as if the baby is not using a bunting but a jacket instead.

Other options:

- Fancy clothing: this is usually purchased on an as-needed basis since situations such as these cannot always be prepared for ahead of time. For a girl, this will usually include something like a dress, a bow, and stockings. For a boy, this would include a suit, shirt, and tie or bow tie.

- Baby bows: this more specific to baby girls and is used mostly for decorative purposes. They come in all sorts of sizes, from small to bows that are larger than the baby's head. Each of them has something special about it. This is not necessarily a practical piece of clothing, but for baby girls, it can be very adorable.

Swimming:

Swimming is a fun past time for both adults and children, and even babies. Though of course, they won't be able to swim just yet, there is nothing that says babies cannot be brought either to a pool or the beach. As is, a baby will need some type of swimsuit to wear, and with so many options it can be overwhelming.

- Rashguard: can be purchased for both boys and girls. This can be either a shirt or a one-piece that resembles a romper. They are made of a specialized material to be used in the sun.

- Swim trunks: are miniature versions of swim trunks that you can buy for an adult. The material is usually made with UPF 50 for sun protection. Most of the time, they will also have a mesh on the inside, however, a baby will still need a diaper (preferably one made for swimming, so it is not as ultra-absorbent as regular diapers).

- One-piece swimsuits: are a great comfortable design for girls, giving them freedom and comfort at the same time.

- Two-piece bikinis: though this is also an option for girls, they may not be the best for a newborn. The reason for this is that babies need to be covered more to be protected from the sun and other elements around them. Purchasing a one-piece instead will keep your baby girl warm and protected at the same time.

Another tip for the sun, whether boy or girl, is to use a sun hat. This will ensure that the baby's face and neck are protected from the sun before they reach an age where they can use suntan lotion. Hats designed for the pool or the beach are also made of a material that is around UPF 50 to ensure that the baby does not get too much sun.

Small tips:

When purchasing any of the baby clothes mentioned above, it is best to keep some things in mind to make the baby as comfortable as possible. Remember, a baby spends most of their time asleep or just laying down and it is best to purchase clothing that will make them comfortable.

- Purchase clothing that is seasonally appropriate such as short sleeves onesies in the summer and long-sleeves in the winter.

- Buy clothing that is comfortable such as no large buttons.

- Avoid clothing with a hood or a collar. This is partly because a hood can get stuck or wrapped around the baby, and the other is due to the fact that both pieces of clothing would touch the baby's cheek. In the beginning, when the baby's cheek is touched it triggers the rooting reflex which would make the baby constantly search for food.

- Unless the opening is big enough, avoid buying things that have to go over the head. This is mostly for your own comfort as parents rather than for the babies. That is to say, keep in mind that anything that is tight going over the head will be tight being taken off which means if the baby has a poop blow-out, you might smear the baby in it unless you want to cut off the piece of clothing. As an added tip, some onesies come with shoulder flaps which extend the neckline and allow the onesie to be taken off through the bottom as opposed to the top.

- It is best to stick to clothing that is soft, easy to clasp (such as buttons on a onesie that are between the legs) with built-in feet. This will minimize the amount of work that has to be done every time that a baby has to have a diaper change and the number of lost socks.

Clothing the baby at the hospital

Depending on how the baby is born, whether vaginal or c-section, will determine the next steps, however, in the end, the baby is always placed into a newborn shirt and a swaddle, with a small hat on for warmth. Though parents are allowed to bring their own outfits, and some choose to, there is actually no need.

Part of the reason that is best to leave the baby in the clothes provided by the hospital is the ease of access. Throughout the day, each day before discharge, nurses will be checking in on the baby to make sure that the baby is doing well. There will also be a pediatrician stopping by at least once a day. By leaving the baby in the hospital shirt and the swaddle blanket, nurses are able to come in and do their job quickly and efficiently without disturbing the baby too much.

If you choose to bring outfits for the baby to the hospital to wear before going home, it is best to keep it simple, such as footed sleepers or onesies. It is best to bring a few just in case there are any diaper accidents. Since the baby will still be swaddled to help them sleep through the newborn startle reflex, they do not have to be overly warm outfits so that the baby does not overheat.

One more thing that the hospital provides is the standard-issue blankets that are white, pink, and blue and have become known almost everywhere. Though parents have been told not to take those home, plenty of them do for sentimental reasons. With the hospitals providing these blankets for generations, they have become a staple of the newborn wardrobe and baby's first pictures. They are also specifically designed to be just the right size and shape to be a swaddle for the baby.

Coming home outfit

Choosing a coming home outfit has become a rather lengthy and involved process, with parents striving to choose the outfit they believe is best. The choice of what to bring the baby home in is completely up to the parents, though some strive to make the outfit more memorable than the rest.

With many companies out there targeting this type of market, there are plenty of choices from practical to adorable. Some parents have even personalized the outfit with the chosen name of the baby, or a small saying or poem.

There is no right or wrong answer, however, what should be kept in mind is that you will never know the exact size that the baby will be born. Unless you plan on purchasing different outfits (or even the same one) in different sizes, it is also good to have a backup in case the baby is either bigger or smaller than was expected.

Even if adorable is what you are going for, remember to keep the baby comfortable as well. Comfort is going to be key for the baby and parents on one of those most important days. Going home is already a new experience for the baby, and can be quite overwhelming, therefore, it is best to make the transition from hospital to home as easy as possible. Also, once the baby is home, most of the time they will end up going back to sleep, so choosing something more comfortable will minimize the amount of fuss needed once there.

To top it off, remember, that this type of outfit will only be worn by the baby most likely once, if not just a small handful of times. Since outfits like these can be pricier than the rest, if money is a factor, it may be best to go with something more practical, which of course can still be flattering and memorable for the occasion.

Tips for dressing a newborn

Dressing a baby for the first time can be an intimidating undertaking, but it can be overcome. Since a newborn is not the wiggle worm that it will once become, the process of dressing a newborn is much easier with some practice. There are a few short tips that can be considered in order to make the process easy in the hospital and at home.

- Dress the baby on a changing table or a wider surface such as a bed or the floor. Once the baby is able to start rolling over, which won't be for a couple of months, it is best to avoid places such as a bed to prevent the baby from taking a tumble, therefore, it might be best to get in the habit of doing it somewhere else right away.

- In the beginning, babies will not be able to pull away from things that cover their faces, so it is best to dress them in clothes that fit the baby and do not wrap around their neck too tight. Make sure that anything decorative such as buttons is secured tightly and won't fall off as the baby is wearing their outfit.

- Due to the wiggly nature of babies, it is best to reach through either the sleeves or the legs before pulling the limb through. This will minimize the chance that the baby may get stuck or hurt.

- Make it a bonding moment. This can be done by talking or singing with the baby. In some instances, it may make the process of getting dressed easier once the baby is bigger and starts to have opinions of their own.

Dressing a baby does not have to be as heart-stopping as it might sound. Babies are a lot tougher than most people think that they are, and with some practice, it is possible to get the hang of it. Parents can become experts in no time and will gladly branch out their baby's wardrobe as time goes on.

Choosing type of diaper; disposable or cloth

The decision whether to use cloth or disposable diapers is another big decision in the life of a parent and, as with many other choices, there is no right or wrong answer. The decision will vary from family to family based on a number of different circumstances which may make one easier to use than the other.

There are no real differences between cloth and disposable diapers except for someone's preference. It is perfectly acceptable to also make that decision once the baby has been born and it is easier to see what the routine will look like and whether it will fit the family. It may also be a better option to wait until the baby's arrival as not all cloth diapers are made equal. Disposable diapers will come in all sorts of sizes and if you find that you have the wrong one, you can either purchase more or exchange what you have. Cloth diapers, on the other hand, start at a certain rage of weight the baby must meet, meaning that they may not work for each baby right away.

One of the biggest decision-making differences between the two is the total cost. The average cost of diapering one child can run up to $3,000 for around two years. The price goes up, of course, if it is taking the baby a little longer to potty train than the moment, they hit two years. However, cloth diapering can run around $1,000 total if you plan on doing laundry yourself. If you plan on outsourcing diaper laundry, the total price will end up running similar to those of disposable diapers.

It is important to remember though, that the total price of the diapers when using cloth has to be paid upfront. This is due to the fact that a newborn will most likely end up being changed around ten times a day. In order to be able to keep up with the demand, you will have to purchase enough diapers to last those ten times for at least two days so that you are not forced to do laundry more than once a day. Of course, if you do not want to, or have the ability to, do laundry once a day, you will end up needing more diapers. This could equate to around twenty to thirty cloth diapers on hand.

If you plan on moving forward with disposable diapers, that cost can be spread out over time allowing you to save for those week by week, but of course, as mentioned earlier, the total cost of the diapering will end up running about twice as much.

The biggest benefit of cloth diapers is that you are able to use them on any subsequent sibling. With the proper care and cleaning, they can last for years and be used for multiple siblings once one is potty trained. In some instances, if parents have decided they are done having children, it is possible to resell them to another set of parents. There are plenty of different platforms that parents frequent, such as Facebook Marketplace, that make it easier to sell such items that are still in good condition.

Since most cloth diapers have a minimum weight recommendation before they fit the baby properly, this is something that can be held off until the baby is born. This will allow you time to decide which ones will work best for you and your family as well as which ones will fit the baby how quickly. If in the meantime you decide that disposable diapering will work better, you have not spent the money on cloth diapering before you were sure of which avenue to take.

Convenience is also something that is a factor when choosing which is the best for your family. Disposable diapers can be move convenient, especially when on the go, therefore, it is good to keep in mind that cloth diapering can be something done strictly at home. However, there are parents who find cloth diapering a little cumbersome. Though cloth diapers have come leaps and bounds from what they used to be back in the day, there are still quite a bit of pieces that need to be juggled in order to make it work.

Disposable diapers are a one and done deal, meaning that they can be thrown out the moment that they've been soiled, straight into the garbage with the entire mess. Sometimes, even the outfit goes with if it was a big enough explosion. That is not the case, however, with cloth diapers. They require washing, but in the meantime, they have to be stored in a bag, or laundry hamper, that is specifically designed to hold those diapers as they are wet and most likely soiled.

A baby can pee up to twenty times a day, and within those twenty breastfed babies will poop at least three times a day and formula-fed babies around one to four times. What this means for the parent, is the need to store all of those diapers in between washes. If parents are on the go, storing and bringing those back home can become quite cumbersome, and some might find it quite gross.

Some have also made the claim that cloth diapers are better for the environment, swaying parents to go down that route. However, that is not as clear cut as it seems. Yes, disposable diapers do fill up landfills and do not always degrade the way that we would like them to, however, cloth diapers require a lot of cleaning which of course requires energy and water.

If it is hard to commit to the purchase of cloth diapers upfront, as you need to make a big enough purchase for the whole thing to make sense, and you do not personally have anyone to ask advice of, there are online and community groups that either provide that much needed advice or testimonials, but also rentals. There are boutiques out there that give the ability to rent diapers in different brands to see which ones would work best when considering cloth diapering. This helps with making the ultimate decision to spend or not spend the money.

The decision on what would work best for the family lies only with the parents, however, there is no right or wrong answer. If you find that cloth diapering is not for you, there is no reason to feel as if there has been a wrong decision made, even though some would make you feel otherwise.

Takeaway

Overall, there are many options out there when it comes to clothing the baby, from what to bring to a hospital, their coming home outfit, how many clothes they should have in the beginning, to whether to include cloth diapers or disposable diapers in the whole ensemble.

Though there are certain guidelines that can be provided, such as the recommended amount of articles of clothing, there are no right or wrong answers when it comes to what the parents decide. Most of the time, it will be trial and error that parents have to learn to cope with. You can purchase or be gifted as many little outfits as you choose, whether your baby ends up wearing them all or not.

You can go either practical or pretty no matter what gender your baby is, and that is quite alright. Many parents, especially mothers, love to dress their child up in special outfits and that is their choice. A baby is a newborn only once in their life and you can make that time special for you, whatever that means.

CHAPTER 7:

Caring for a Circumcision

Circumcision is a very personal decision that should not be influenced by anyone, but it has become a highly volatile topic among parents. It is, of course, a decision that can in no way be reversed, but should be discussed before the birth of the baby, even if the gender is not known right away.

Though statistics vary by region, in the United States around 55% to 65% of all newborn baby boys undergo circumcision. This is a procedure that is common mostly in North America, Africa, and the Middle East. It is not a common procedure performed in South America, Asia, or Europe.

If the baby is being born in the hospital, the decision on whether to circumcise or not should be made known to the hospital nurse. As it is the ob-gyn that will perform the procedure most likely within a day or two of the birth, they will be made aware immediately.

If the baby is not being born in the hospital, contact your pediatrician for further guidance on how to set up the procedure. It is best, however, not to wait too long if you would like to have your boy circumcised since the longer you wait, the more painful it is.

First, what is it and why?

What is it?

Anatomically, boys are born with a layer of skin called the foreskin covering the head of the penis that is called the glans. Circumcision is the surgical removal of the foreskin of the penis. This is the layer of skin that covers the head of the penis. It is a straight forward procedure that is performed by the obstetric gynecologist that delivered the baby if the delivery was in the hospital.

Usually, this procedure is performed within the first ten days of the baby's life to minimize any risks and pain, though usually if the baby is born in hospital doctors try to do it within a day or two.

The choice to have a son circumcised can vary greatly, but some of the most common reasons are:

- Health benefit: specifically, the prevention of urinary tract infections (UTI) as well as the decreased possibility of contracting sexually transmitted diseases

(STD). For uncircumcised males, there are bacteria that get caught underneath the skin which can lead to UTI. It is believed that with the removal of that skin, there is a fewer risk of having a UTI. There has also been research performed which came to the conclusion that males that have been circumcised have a smaller chance of contracting HIV from an infected partner, however, as with most things, more research is still needed.

- Appearance: if, for instance, the father of the child has been circumcised, parents might be more inclined to do the same in order to make sure that they do not look different.

- Religion or culture: in some cultures, or religions, circumcision is something that has been a part of the practice for many centuries, for example, in the Muslim or Jewish communities.

Why not?

Some parents choose not to move forward with circumcision, due to:

- Pain: parents decide not to have this procedure done to spare the baby any pain as this is something that will have to heal over some time. Though the baby is given an anesthetic before the procedure itself takes place, it is still a wound that has to heal when the baby is taken home.

- Risk: as with any other surgical procedure, there is also a risk when circumcising a child. Though they are very rare, complications are something that can happen and will include either bleeding, infection or scarring. To mitigate these types of problems, it is best to ensure that it is a medical professional who is well trained in this procedure that will carry out the circumcision.

- Autonomy: some parents believe that this is a decision that should be made by the child once they are old enough to make it, however, this is something that is quite painful to do once the child is older, especially as they are nearing adulthood. At that time, there is also a bigger possibility of complications arising.

Methods

To assist you in the decision on whether to have your boy circumcised, it is best to familiarize yourself with the different methods that the procedure is performed. These methods are through the use of the Gomco circumcision clamp, the Mogen circumcision clamp, or the PlastiBell circumcision device. In the U.S. however, the Gomco clamp is one of the most commonly used devices, but you can always check that with the doctor that will be performing the procedure.

- Of the three types of devices, the Gomco clamp is one of the most difficult to use even if it provides better cosmetic results. It is the hardest because the partially cut foreskin must be threaded between the bell and the clamp before the actual clamp is tightened to make the cut. This also comes with some bleeding.

- The Mogen clamp is the next most commonly used and mostly within the Jewish community. This device is the one that is generally regarded as the quickest and the one that produces the least discomfort.

- The PlastiBell is very easy in its use, but it must remain on the penis until the foreskin becomes necrotic and it falls off. This process may take seven to ten days which means that many parents tend to dislike this type of device.

Electrocautery is the one type of method that is not recommended which is something commonly used by urologists. This is not a recommended method due to the studies that have been performed which revealed that there are possible complications such as the transected penile head (or cut), severe burns, or meatal stenosis (a narrowing of the urethral opening, or the hole at the top).

Knowing what the procedure looks like beforehand may ease the decision-making process one way or another. Some parents are afraid to make the decision because they never know what they are getting in to, but that should have eased the picture that the mind creates when it comes to circumcision.

The Checklist

Before a circumcision is performed there are a couple of things that have to be checked off the proverbial checklist to ensure that it is safe to have it performed. Usually, these things are done by the doctor, but as parents, it is also good to keep on top of the process from start to finish.

- The baby must be examined by a pediatrician or another doctor who can provide the same level of care to determine that all is well.

- The baby must be full-term (or close to) how is healthy and has been stable.

- The penis itself must be of normal size without any defects.

- It must be determined by the doctor that if the procedure is carried out, the skin of the shaft does not move forward to cover the head of the penis due to excess abdominal fat.

- Determine that there is no risk of a bleeding disorder that may prove counterproductive to the correct healing of the circumcision.

- A vitamin K shot must have been administered to the baby upon birth to help with clotting.

The How

The circumcision procedure lasts usually no more than ten minutes and is done within ten days of the baby's birth in the nursery. The quick procedure will see that your son is lying on his back with arms and legs restrained to prevent undue movement. The doctor will inject an anesthetic into the base of the penis after the area has been fully cleansed. Sometimes the anesthetic is actually provided in the form of a cream.

Once the foreskin is removed with whichever method your doctor has deemed best, the penis will be covered with a topic antibiotic or some petroleum jelly and wrapped in gauze.

For boys or adults that are older, the procedure looks much the same, however, it might be performed under general anesthesia and it might take longer to heal. There are also greater risks of different complications taking place in older males, hence why the push for it to be done when the baby is born.

Caring for the circumcision

Due to the fact that circumcision is a surgical procedure, it will require a certain level of care once it is performed. This is to ensure that the risk of contracting any infections is minimized and that it heals without needing any medical intervention. Normally, the staff at the hospital where it is done will go through the process with you, however, here are things to keep in mind.

- During each diaper change, without touching it as much as is possible, inspect the penis to see that it does not appear infected.

- No thorough cleaning will need to be performed so as not to cause any undue pain.

- Before replacing the diaper, apply a liberal amount of petroleum jelly either straight on to the penis or on to a gauze that you will place over the penis inside the diaper. This is to ensure that the wound does not dry out or get stuck to the fabric of the diaper.

- If any stool does get on to the penis, since as a newborn stool can be very loose, use a soft cotton towel and nothing more than soap and water to clean off the dirty area.

- Usually, circumcision will be healed fully within about seven to ten days. In the meantime, you will find that the head of the penis will appear red and there will be what looks like a yellow fluid. Both of these are quite normal as the penis heals from the procedure.

- If during your inspection you find that the penis is not healing within the specified amount of time, has turned a different color, or has crusted over, it is best to contact the pediatrician office immediately for further instructions.

Once the penis has healed from the procedure, cleaning it on a daily basis will require nothing more than soap and water during bath time. If during a diaper change, you find that the stool has made its way up, a wet wipe will suffice.

If you find that there is some skin left over, do not attempt to pull the skin back on your own as this could cause more harm than good. Most of the time this skin will detach on its own as it does for a boy who has been left uncircumcised. If there are any questions on the way that it healed, or if it looks correct, ask the pediatrician.

What if I don't do it?

If you choose to not circumcise your son, let your wishes be known at the hospital while you are being admitted for delivery. It is best to ensure that all medical staff is aware of your request, however, no one should move forward with any procedures as you would have to sign your approval.

The care for an uncircumcised penis is a little different overall, however, it is not any more difficult than if the procedure was done.

- When dirty, such as during a runny stool, wash the penis with soap and water, nothing else is required.

- Do not under any circumstances, pull back on the foreskin. This used to be advised to new parents, however, it was found to be doing more harm to boys than it was beneficial. It's important to remember that most likely the skin will not fully pull back until the boy is older.

- As your boy ages, remember to teach him the importance of washing the area with soap and water as by that point in time he should be able to gently start moving the foreskin back to clean properly.

There is nothing wrong with leaving a boy uncircumcised. Studies have shown that more parents are starting to shy away from the practice for various reasons. The care for a penis that has not been circumcised is not any more difficult as mentioned below as there are only key pieces to remember.

Takeaway

Circumcision is a personal choice on the part of the parents and as with everything else, there is technically no right answer. Above are some of the key points on what circumcision is and what it looks like as well as the criteria the baby boy needs to meet before having it performed.

Since it is a surgery, it is best to discuss all the information that you have learned with the doctor who will be performing the surgery such as the ob-gyn or the pediatrician. If you choose to move forward, the medical staff at the hospital will teach you how to care for the wound once you go home, but it does not take long to heal at all. Within ten days or so, everything has healed and will no longer require any special care.

If you choose to uncircumcised, there are no other steps that need to be done besides educating yourself on how to care for it during bath time or diaper changes. Nowadays, it is best to leave the skin as is, as it will finally retract on its own as the boy grows and that is the most important thing to remember. Again, this is something that can be asked the hospital staff before going home with the baby for the first time.

CONCLUSION

Thank you for making it through to the end of *Newborn Care Basics: Baby Care Tips For New Moms*, let's hope it was informative and able to provide you with all of the tools you need to achieve your goals whatever they may be. As with many topics, there is a wealth of information out there to learn, with this book being just the beginning.

The next step is to further your knowledge on any of the topics listed above such as discussing important information with your chosen pediatrician or ob-gyn. There are other books available online or at your local library, as well as community groups that could point you in the right direction. Don't be afraid to reach out and generate more information that you could use later.

The most important thing to remember when caring for a newborn is that not everything is a one size fits all. Not every baby is the same just as not every parent is the same, and there is nothing wrong with that. Based on the knowledge that you have gained after reading this book, choose the options that best suit the needs of your baby and your family. Be it, the type of clothes you choose, whether you move forward with cloth or disposable diapers, or bathe your baby daily. As a parent, you will no doubt do your best and continue to learn things along the way that will help you bond with your baby and watch them continue to grow beyond the newborn stage.

Do let us know how this book helped you by leaving a review. This will encourage eager parents to make the right purchase.

Happy Parenting!

OTHER BOOKS BY LISA MARSHALL

Easy Newborn Care Tips

Proven Parenting Tips For Your Newborn's Development, Sleep Solution And Complete Feeding Guide

Toddler Discipline Tips

The Complete Parenting Guide With Proven Strategies To Understand And Managing Toddler's Behavior, Dealing With Tantrums, And Reach an Effective Communication Communication With Kids

*** Subscribe to Our Newsletter
and Get a <u>FREE</u> Audiobook***

Subscribe to the newsletter and receive a free Audiobook in Positive Parenting series at your choice. Simply email me to let me know which of my books you would like, and I'll send you a promo code you can redeem FREE!

**SUBSCRIBE HERE
https://bit.ly/2FAGaqX**

Note: If you have purchased the paperback format then you need to write this link on your browser search bar.

Finally, if you found this book useful in any way, a review on Amazon is always appreciated!

Made in the USA
Coppell, TX
22 February 2020

16102160R00083